music

AN A-Z GUIDE

WRITTEN BY

NICOLA BARBER

FRANKLIN WATTS

A Division of Scholastic Inc.

New York   Toronto   London   Auckland   Sydney

Mexico City   New Delhi   Hong Kong

Produced in association with **ticktock** *publishing ltd.*

Writer: *Nicola Barber*
Editor: *Jeremy Smith*
Managing Editor: *Penny Worms*
Designers: *Graham Rich, Rod Teasdale*

Library of Congress Cataloging-in-Publication Data

Barber, Nicola.
Music: an A-Z guide / Nicky Barber.
p.cm.—(Watts reference)
Includes bibliographical references and index.
ISBN 0-531-11898-3 (lib. bdg.)   0-531-15450-5 (pbk.)
1. Music—Dictionaries, Juvenile. [1. Music—Dictionaries.] I. Title. II. Series.
ML 100. B265 2001
780'.3—dc21
00-051325

CONTENTS

CONTENTS

INTRODUCTION

by Jason Polise

As a performer and composer, I witness first-hand the sheer power that music can have on an audience. Music has the very unique ability to bring out characteristics of our personality or mood. Because music has such a tremendous impact on our mood, it can be used to alter or change our state of mind. Movies are a clear example of how closely an audience's emotions can be tied to the music.

Most often, the sole purpose for music in a movie is to enhance the desired mood of each scene. It is usually designed to add either suspense or drama. Film composers or film scorers, as they are commonly referred to, craft these mood-setting pieces by selecting certain combinations of instruments and sounds. Very often, music is presented early in a film. This musical theme usually returns several times throughout the movie, changing a little each time. As an audience, use of music in this way gives us a feeling of familiarity with the characters or the setting. As the film progresses, the main theme may be altered to signal a change in the hero's attitude or mood. Great acting accompanied by a good piece of music is often enough to express the idea of the scene without any dialogue at all. I recommend that people, when given the opportunity, watch an exciting film, such as *Star Wars* or *Jurassic Park,* without the music. The results are startling—much of the emotion we experience in a movie is actually brought on by the music.

As listeners, we have the freedom to approach music with a very indulgent attitude, listening to an entire piece of music or just our favorite part. We can focus on our favorite instrument or take in the sound of the entire group. To remain effective at invoking emotions, music has had to evolve to match the changing attitudes of both listeners and performers. People today listen to an enormous range of musical styles, from classical and jazz to rock and rap.

Music: An A-Z Guide gives a comprehensive overview of the world of music in its various forms today. Alphabetical entries cover all facets of music, from the technical aspects of musical performance to the genres that entertain listeners around the globe. Several entries have song lists that will help readers get acquainted with key performers from each genre.

Music has the ability to inspire, to empower, and is, contrary to common belief, absolutely not reserved for the talented few. Whether you are a listener or a musician, keep this book nearby, as it will be an indispensable tool on your musical journey.

A graduate of the Eastman School of Music, Jason Polise teaches music at Middlesex Middle School in Darien, Connecticut.

ACOUSTICS

Acoustics is the science of sound: how sound is produced, how it travels, and how it is heard. The term is also used to refer to the technology of sound; for example the design of musical instruments or sound-producing equipment. The word acoustics is often used to describe the quality of sound in a room, such as an auditorium or a library.

The Science of Sound

The acoustics of a room are affected by many different factors, including its size and shape and the materials used in its construction. This concert hall in Minneapolis is designed specifically for orchestras. It takes advantage of the most up-to-date materials to make the most of sound. The hard, domed surface of the ceiling helps to direct the sound back down to the audience, while the curved wall behind the orchestra acts as a concave reflecter, ensuring that sound waves are not trapped behind the performers.

Sound Waves

When a sound is made, sound waves travel out in all directions. When these sound waves hit a surface, some bounce off while some are absorbed. Some surfaces are more absorbent than others. When engineers are designing auditoriums, they have to think about the kind of materials they are using. Hard materials such as stone reflect sound well, but a large space made from stone, such as a cathedral, produces too many echoes to hear music or words clearly. Equally, a room full of soft materials, such as carpets and thick curtains, will absorb a lot of the waves, making the sound very muffled. The secret of good acoustics lies in creating the right balance.

• See also pages 81, 105

ANCIENT INSTRUMENTS

Some musical instruments have been played for thousands of years. We know about many of these instruments from wall paintings and from objects buried in ancient tombs. Some were very simple, such as rattles. Many of these primitive instruments are still played today.

Doing the Didjeridu

The didjeridu is an ancient instrument from Australia, played by the Australian Aboriginal people. It is made from the branch of a eucalyptus tree, the center of which has been hollowed out by insects called termites. The tube can be up to 6 feet (2 meters) long. It is played by blowing down one end with vibrating lips, much like playing the trumpet. It produces a very deep, resonant sound. Didjeridus are prized in Aboriginal culture and are often highly decorated.

Shaking and Rattling

These colorful basketwork shakers called caxixi come from Latin America. Basketwork shakers are found throughout Central and South America, and in Africa. The simplest are made from dried flower pods or gourds which contain seeds that rattle. Others are made from clay, metal, and wood.

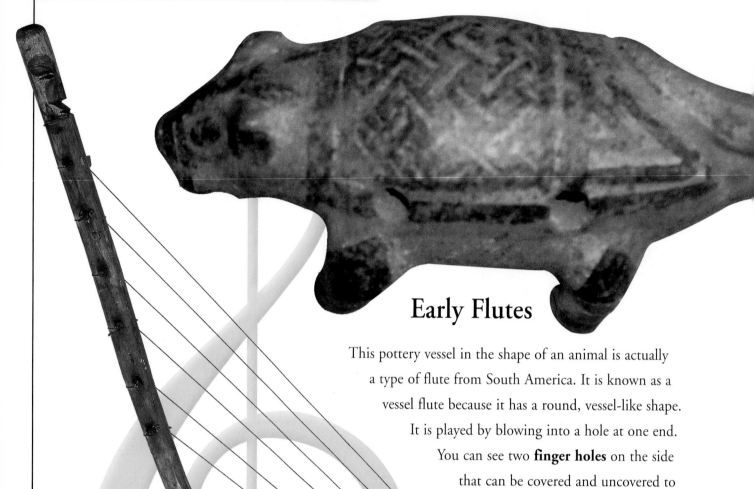

Early Flutes

This pottery vessel in the shape of an animal is actually a type of flute from South America. It is known as a vessel flute because it has a round, vessel-like shape. It is played by blowing into a hole at one end. You can see two **finger holes** on the side that can be covered and uncovered to make different **notes**. Modern vessel flutes are called ocarinas.

Ancient Bows

This bow harp comes from Africa. It has six **strings** attached at one end to a neck, and at the other end to a gourd (a dried vegetable shell) which magnifies the sound. Bow harps are found throughout Africa and eastern Asia. They evolved from the musical bow, one of the oldest instruments in the world.

Clapping the Clappers

One of the simplest ways to produce a sound is to strike two objects together. These two hand-shaped clappers would each have formed one half of an identical pair. They come from Ancient Egypt and they are over 3,000 years old. They were probably used during ceremonies as an alternative to clapping the hands together.

The Sound of the Shofar

This rabbi is playing a shofar, an ancient horn that has been part of the Jewish tradition for thousands of years. This simple instrument is crafted from the horn of a ram. The horn is straightened and hollowed out, and is usually played with a separate **mouthpiece** that is fitted over the end. The shofar can produce two different **notes**. It is still sounded during Jewish feasts such as Yom Kippur, the Day of Atonement.

● *See also pages 38, 82*

BAGPIPES

Ancient manuscripts reveal that bagpipes have been played since Roman times. Different styles of bagpipes developed all over Europe, but the best-known today are the Great Highland Bagpipes which come from Scotland. While not everyone warms to the sound of these famous pipes, their evocative **tone** is known all over the world.

How Bagpipes Work

Bagpipes are played by blowing through a blowpipe into a bag, or by working a pair of small bellows under the player's arm. When the air-filled bag is squeezed, the air flows out through pipes attached to the bag. One of these pipes, the **chanter**, has **finger holes** to change the **pitch** of the **note**. This is the pipe used to play **melodies**. The **drone** (some bagpipes have more than one) sounds as a continuous note that does not change.

DRONE

BLOW PIPE

BAG

CHANTER

The Highland Bagpipes

This Scottish piper is wearing traditional Highland dress and playing the Great Highland Bagpipes. You can see the blowpipe, chanter, and three drones. Bagpipes are an important part of many European folk cultures. The bags are usually made from sheep or goatskin, and are often beautifully decorated.

• See also pages 38, 79, 88

Ballet music is music that is designed to reflect and complement the dance that accompanies it. It is a romantic, passionate music that often tells a story on its own. An atmosphere is created so that you can get a sense of what is happening even without watching the dance.

On Stage

The movements of dancers in time to music are worked out by a person called a **choreographer**. Sometimes the composer and choreographer work very closely together to create a ballet. The Russian composer Peter Ilyich Tchaikovsky worked with the Russian choreographer Pepita on his ballets. It is said that, for some passages, Pepita even told Tchaikovsky how many **bars** of music to write to ensure that the music was just right for her dancers!

Peter Ilyich Tchaikovsky (1840–93)

Born in Votkinsk in Russia, the young Tchaikovsky studied law before taking up music. He went to the St. Petersburg Conservatory where he was taught by the great pianist Anton Rubinstein. Tchaikovsky began to write music seriously when he was about 26. He composed three ballets: Swan Lake, The Nutcracker, *and* Sleeping Beauty. *Tchaikovsky traveled widely, and by the time of his death in 1893, he had become a well-known and successful composer.*

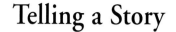

Telling a Story

Imagine a ballet without music. The movements of the dancers would mean nothing without the stirring accompaniment of a classical orchestra. Since the early beginnings of ballet in the 1500s, many composers have written music especially for ballets, including Tchaikovsky and his fellow countryman Igor Stravinsky. The music in the classical ballet *Sleeping Beauty* creates the magical, fairy-tale atmosphere appropriate for the story it accompanies. In "The Dance of the Sugar-Plum Fairy" in *The Nutcracker* ballet, Tchaikovsky created an air of magic and mystery using an instrument called a celesta, an instument with a keyboard and metal plates specially built for the production. When struck, the plates produced a bell-like tone.

Modern Dance

Modern ballet began in the 1920s when, influenced by the work of Picasso and sculptors such as Henry Moore, dancers such as Martha Graham and Mary Wigman began to dance in sculptural, angular forms. They rejected their traditional costume, and began to

perform barefoot in strikingly different dress. This picture shows the ballet company Philadanco performing in New York in 1999. Other dance companies like the Ballet Rambert perform to popular rather than classical music.

• *See also page 27*

BASSOON

The bassoon was developed in the 17th century, and became part of the European orchestra during the 18th century. Early versions had **finger holes** and a few very simple keys, but the modern bassoon has keys covering all its finger holes. The most famous bassoon-maker is the German family firm, Heckel, which started making instruments in 1831. Heckel bassoons are still prized today.

Playing the Bassoon

The bassoon is quite a heavy instrument, so the player either wears a sling around the neck to relieve some of the weight, or uses a spike to rest the instrument on the floor. It is played with a double **reed**, which is fitted onto the end of a metal tube called the **crook**. Players can buy reeds, but many choose to make their own. Bassoons are made from wood, often maple.

Contra-bassoon

The contra-bassoon is also known as the double bassoon. It has a tube 18 feet (5 ½ meters) long, bent back on itself. The tube of the normal bassoon is about half this length. The bassoon is the bass instrument in the woodwind section of the orchestra, but it is sometimes heard as a solo instrument. The contra-bassoon sounds an **octave** lower than the bassoon.

● *See also pages 116-117*

13

BLUES

The blues is a type of music that developed in the southern United States. This lamenting style of music started to become popular in the early 1900s, and the first recordings were made in the 1920s. The blues was a very important influence on many later types of music, particularly jazz.

Early Blues

The blues comes from the songs of early African-Americans who were forced to work as slaves in the cotton plantations of the South. Some of these tunes were work songs, others were field **hollers**, so called because workers called out to each other across the plantations in order to break the monotony of the work. The other early influence on the blues were Christian hymns. At first, blues songs were sung without accompaniment, but gradually people began to play along with the songs on guitar.

Playing the Blues

This man is playing the banjo, an instrument developed by African-American slaves on the plantations. The banjo was made from a wooden hoop with a piece of animal skin stretched tightly across, acting as a **sound box**. Blues songs were often melancholy, reflecting on life's troubles. One of their characteristic sounds was "blue **notes**." These were certain notes in the **scale** that were slightly flattened to give the music a sorrowful quality.

Bessie Smith (1894–1937)

Bessie Smith was born into a poor family in Chattanooga, Tennessee. She was discovered in her teens by a record producer, and quickly became one of the best-known blues singers of the 1920s. She made recordings with jazz legends including Louis Armstrong and Fletcher Henderson, and was known as "Empress of the Blues." Bessie Smith died from injuries she received in a car accident in 1937.

Blues Tunes

1. *Everyday I Have The Blues*
   Count Basie
2. *When Love Comes To Town*
   B.B. King
3. *Johnny B. Goode*
   Chuck Berry
4. *Georgia On My Mind*
   Ray Charles
5. *Layla*
   Eric Clapton
6. *Just The Same*
   Dr. John
7. *Boom Boom*
   John Lee Hooker
8. *Spoonful*
   Howlin' Wolf
9. *Weak Brain, Narrow Mind*
   Willie Dixon
10. *Feel Like Going Home*
    Muddy Waters

1. E	2. E	3. E	4. E
5. A	6. A	7. E	8. E
9. B	10. A	11. E	12. B

The 12-bar Blues

In the early 1900s, the blues developed into a recognizable musical form with its own structure and particular sound. Many blues songs were based on a pattern of 12 **bars**, with a sequence of **chords** similar to the blues in the **key** of E, shown here. The 12 bars were usually divided into three sections of four bars. The words of the first section were often repeated in the second section, with a response in the third section.

• *See also page 104*

BRASS FAMILY

The brass family is made up of the French horn, trumpet, trombone, and tuba, as well as the euphonium, cornet, bugle, and sousaphone. All these instruments are made from metal—although not necessarily brass!

Brass Instruments

This picture shows the brass section of a brass band. At the back you can see a row of tubas. In front is the euphonium section. In a classical orchestra, the brass section is made up of trumpets, trombones, French horns, and tubas.

Seating Of A Modern Orchestra

French Horns   Trumpets   Trombones and Tubas

The brass section usually sits towards the back of the orchestra, behind the woodwind section.

Bugle

The bugle is a simple brass instrument which can be played using one hand. It was used in medieval times to rally huntsmen, but in the late 18th century, it began to be used in European armies as a signalling instrument. Some bugles have **valves** (see page 112), but many are valveless. They are played by altering the pressure of the lips in the **mouthpiece** to produce different **pitches**. In the United States, larger bugles are also made to be played in military bugle bands.

In the Workshop

This picture shows the inside of a 17th century brass instrument-maker's workshop. The craftsman is working at a conical tube to fashion a trombone. Hanging on the wall on the right is a large circular horn and below it a trumpet. The first trombones we know about were played at the end of the 15th century. They were called sackbuts. These early brass instruments did not have valves, which were first added in the 19th century. The player sounded different **notes** by changing the pressure of the lips and air flow.

• *See also pages 59, 60, 109*

CELLO

The cello (or violincello) is a member of the string family. It was developed in the 16th century as a kind of "bass violin," and is both an important member of the classical orchestra and a solo instrument in its own right. The cello is played by world-famous performers such as Julian Lloyd Webber and Yo-Yo Ma.

Playing the Cello

The cello is positioned between the player's knees, and is balanced on the floor with a metal spike. A full-size cello measures about four feet (15 meters) in length, but there are smaller cellos for children who are starting to learn how to play. Its beautifully deep and sensuous **tone** has encouraged composers from J.S. Bach to Edward Elgar to write famous pieces for the cello.

Yo-Yo Ma (1955–)

The cellist Yo-Yo Ma was born in Paris in 1955 to Chinese parents. He studied at the Juilliard School of Music in New York, and now enjoys a successful international career playing with the world's major orchestras. Ma draws his inspiration from a wide range of music. He has studied the music and instruments of China, and the folk traditions of the people who live along the "Silk Road," the ancient trading route that connects Asia and Europe. Ma plays a Stradivari cello that once belonged to another famous cellist, Jacqueline du Pré.

• See also pages 106–107

Chamber music describes music written for small groups of musicians. The term came into use in the 16th century, when musical **ensembles** played for wealthy patrons in private homes. Today, the term is usually used to describe music where each musical **part** is played by just one person as opposed to orchestral pieces where several people play the same part.

A Chamber Concert

This painting, dating from the 1750s, shows a concert at the court of Prince Bishop Luettich at Seraing Palace in Bavaria. Two musicians are playing a viol (a flat-backed violin played with a curved bow), accompanied by a female harpsichord player. The Prince Bishop, his family, and guests surround the players for this private concert. Musicians of this period relied on wealthy patrons such as the Prince Bishop for their livelihoods.

The Brodsky Quartet

Chamber music is very popular today, and can be regularly heard in concert halls around the world. One of the best-known string quartets is the Brodsky Quartet. Unusually, they always play standing up (except for the cellist). They are one of the groups responsible for breaking down the barrier between "classical" and popular music, performing with pop stars such as Paul McCartney and Björk, as well as the jazz pianist and composer Dave Brubeck.

Josef Haydn (1732–1809)

Austrian-born Josef Haydn began his musical career at the court of Prince Esterhazy, a Hungarian nobleman. He remained at the Esterhazy court for nearly 30 years, in charge of all the music and musicians in the household. His tasks included writing music for Prince Esterhazy's enjoyment. He wrote **symphonies** *and* **operas**, *as well as a vast amount of chamber music, mostly for string quartet. In 1790, Prince Esterhazy died, and Haydn moved away from the court, first to Vienna and then to London where he became a huge success.*

Wind Quintet (flute, clarinet, French horn, bassoon, and oboe)

String Quartet (2 violins, viola, and cello)

Chamber groups

Over the centuries, composers have written music for many different combinations of chamber groups. You can see a few of the most common here. There are many pieces of music written for a solo instrument, such as a violin, flute, or clarinet, with piano accompaniment. In the Classical period of European music, music for **string** trios and string quartets was extremely popular. The string quartet has remained important into the 20th century, with composers such as Bela Bartok writing for this combination.

String Trio (violin, viola, and cello)

Solo instrument and piano accompaniment

• See also pages 25-26

Achoir is a group that sings together, with or without accompaniment. Music written for a choir is known as choral music. There are many different kinds of choral groups around the world, including gospel choirs, large choruses that sing with **symphony** orchestras, barbershop groups, and children's choirs.

Barbershop

Barbershop music started in the 18th century when customers waiting for a haircut at the barbers would sing or play music to pass the time. It is an unaccompanied style of singing (also known as a cappella). The lead voice carries the **melody**, and the others sing in close harmony around it. There are usually four singers—traditionally men, although both men and women enjoy barbershop singing today. Barbershop groups are very popular in the United States, and the style of singing has influenced many modern groups, including Boyz II Men and Backstreet Boys.

Gospel Choir

Gospel singing is renowned for its free and joyous sound. Gospel singing developed in the United States in the 19th century, but its roots go much farther back. It draws heavily from "spirituals," plantation songs sung by African-American slaves. These songs were often about the problems of their lives (for example "Nobody Knows The Trouble I Seen").

Gospel also draws on the folk music of the South, the African traditions of the slaves, and the hymns of the Christian Church. Today it is a vital and thriving part of worship across America.

Church Choir

There is a long tradition of cathedral and church choirs, made up of men and women with a range of different pitched voices. Choirs are often made up entirely of boys, admired for the purity of the sound of their voices. Boys enter the choir as young as seven, and stay until their voices break in their early teens. This is the choir of Westminster Cathedral in London rehearsing for a service.

• *See also pages 84, 85, 91, 93*

The clarinet was invented by a German instrument-maker called J.C. Denner in the early 18th century. The clarinet has a single **reed** attached to its **mouthpiece**. It became an established member of the woodwind section in the early 19th century. The clarinet is a very versatile instrument, equally at home in the orchestra and in jazz groups.

Playing the Clarinet

The modern clarinet is made in four parts, usually out of wood. It has a system of **keys** to cover its **finger holes**, some of which are open keys, which are covered by the fingers. When the player blows air into the mouthpiece, the single reed vibrates, producing the smooth **tone** for which the clarinet is appreciated. The clarinet has been made in a number of different sizes.

Benny Goodman (1909–1986)

Benny Goodman was one of 12 children born into a poor Jewish family in Chicago. By the age of 14 he was making his living as a clarinettist. He became a famous bandleader and clarinet player, starting the craze for big band **swing** that earned him the title of the "King of Swing." His bands were among the first to include both black and white musicians.

• See also pages 116-117

CLASSICAL MUSIC

Classical music got its start in Europe between 1725 and 1800 and it continues to thrive today. During the classical era, great composers, such as Mozart and Beethoven, wrote music that emphasized balance, clarity, and moderation. Their complex compositions formed the foundation of what we now consider classical music. Examples of this music style include symphonies, concertos, and chamber music.

Noble Minstrels

During the Middle Ages in Europe, musicians of noble birth wrote poetry and set their words to music. In France these aristocratic musicians were called troubadours; in Germany they were known as minnesingers. This picture dates from 1340 and shows a minnesinger called Kanzler accompanied by two instrumentalists. The minnesingers wrote poems and songs that told stories. The troubadours often wrote poetry about love and chivalry.

Presenting a Mass

This picture is the title page of a Mass setting (a musical arrangement for a Roman Catholic mass service) by the Italian composer Giovanni Pierluigi da Palestrina. It shows the composer presenting his work to the pope in 1554. Palestrina wrote 104 settings of the Mass to be sung at services. He worked in Rome for his whole life, and ran one of the choirs in St. Peter's in the Vatican, the center of the Roman Catholic Church.

Bach in Leipzig

This picture shows the church of St. Thomas in Leipzig, Germany. It was the workplace of Johann Sebastian Bach, one of the greatest composers of all time. Bach came from an extraordinarily musical family—more than a hundred Bachs were involved with music in previous and succeeding generations. He worked in Leipzig for over 25 years, teaching at the school of St. Thomas and writing a steady stream of music for the church. It was here that he wrote some of his best-known works, including the St. John and St. Matthew Passions, and the great B Minor Mass.

Young Prodigies

It was clear from a very early age that Wolfgang Amadeus Mozart was a musical prodigy. His sister, Anna Maria, was also extremely talented, and this picture shows the two children, accompanied by their father. Mozart and his sister traveled widely as children, playing at royal courts all over Europe. Mozart never gained the support of a wealthy patron, and was one of the first composers to live independently off his work. He wrote a vast amount in his short life, including **operas**, **symphonies**, chamber music, and music for the church. He died at the age of 35.

A Musical Evening

Seated at the piano in this picture is Franz Schubert, surrounded by an admiring audience. These private concerts in early 19th-century Vienna were known as "Schubertiads"—when a group of friends gathered to hear the composer's latest work. Schubert wrote more than 600 "lieders," the German word for compositions that set poetry to music. His first song, "Gretchen at the Spinning Wheel," was written when he was just 17, and showed how much drama can be expressed by a voice with piano accompaniment.

Ludwig van Beethoven (1770–1827)

Beethoven was born in Bonn, Germany, to a father who had great ambitions for his son. When Beethoven moved to Vienna in 1792, he quickly became known as a brilliant virtuoso pianist. Tragically, Beethoven's success as a performer was cut short as he gradually became more and more deaf. He stopped performing in public in 1815 but continued to compose until the end of his life. He wrote nine famous **symphonies**, one **opera**, and many pieces of music for chamber groups (see pages 23–24).

Rehearsing with Stravinsky

The Russian composer Igor Stravinsky is pictured in this cartoon rehearsing his work "The Rite of Spring." This ballet was first performed in Paris in 1913. Its spiky **rhythms** and unusual sounds, as well as the passionate dancing of the Ballet Russe, provoked a chorus of jeering and shouting during the performance among an audience used to more conventional, sedate music. In the 1930s, Stravinsky moved to the United States, settling in Hollywood. There he wrote his "Symphony of Psalms," as well as the opera *The Rake's Progress.*

Classical Tunes

1. *The Four Seasons*
   Antonio Vivaldi
2. *Magnificat*
   J.S. Bach
3. *Messiah*
   G.F. Handel
4. *Clarinet Quintet*
   W.A. Mozart
5. *9th Symphony*
   L. van Beethoven
6. *Trout Quintet*
   Franz Schubert
7. *Fantastic Symphony*
   Hector Berlioz
8. *Thus Spoke Zarathustra*
   R. Strauss
9. *Peter and the Wolf*
   S. Prokofiev
10. *Appalachian Spring*
    A. Copland

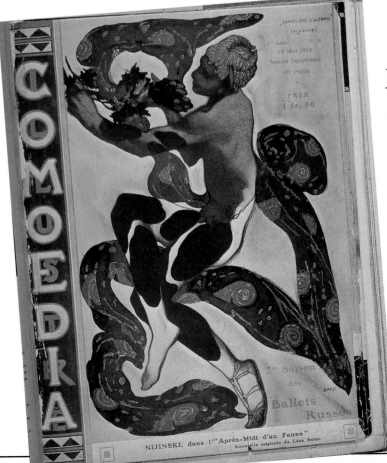

NIJINSKI, dans l'"Après-Midi d'un Faune"
Aquarelle originale de Léon Bakst.

Music for the Ballet

This program cover is for a performance of French composer Claude Debussy's "L'Après-Midi d'un Faune" ("The Afternoon of a Faun"). Debussy was inspired to write this piece by a poem about a faun, a mythical creature that is half-man, half-goat. The music was made into a ballet, and the leading part was taken by the Russian dancer Vaslav Nijinski, shown here. The sound of Indonesian **gamelan** music was a major influence on Debussy, and he made use of its shifting sounds in much of his music.

27

• See also pages 11, 12

COMPUTER MUSIC

Computers can be used to create an endless variety of sounds. If you feed a series of sounds into a computerized musical instrument, such as a synthesizer, you can then alter the sounds in almost any way you like to get your desired effect. This is called **sampling**. Computers can also be used to write music down quickly and efficiently.

Jean-Michel Jarre

The French musician Jean-Michel Jarre has become famous for his experiments with electronic music, and for his extravagant concerts which feature lasers, fireworks, and huge special effects. In 1990, over two and a half million people watched him perform in Paris on Bastille Day (July 14). He had his first hit in 1977 with the album "Oxygène," followed a year later by "Equinoxe." This concert was staged in London's Docklands area.

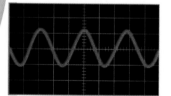 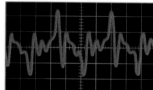

Sampling

Sampling means recording a sound by computer and processing it to create new sounds. Computer waves like the one above on the left make only simple sounds, but more complicated ones like the one above on the right produce much more interesting sounds, like those of real instruments.

Composing at the Computer

This girl is playing a keyboard which is linked to a computer. Using special music software, she can compose directly onto the screen. When she has finished a piece, or a section of a piece, she can print it out or play it back. In the early 1980s, manufacturers agreed to use a standard connection, called **MIDI** (Musical Instrument Digital Interface), to connect computers and electronic musical instruments.

Electronic Experiments

The German composer Karlheinz Stockhausen, seen here at an electronic keyboard, is one of the most important figures in the history of electronic music. Many of the techniques used by musicians today, such as sampling, were first pioneered by Stockhausen. One of his landmark compositions, "Gesang der Jünglinge" ("Song of the Young Boy"), was first heard in the 1950s. It was originally written to be "performed" by five groups of loudspeakers. Stockhausen blended the sound of a boy's voice reciting and singing words from the Bible with a variety of electronic sounds.

COUNTRY AND WESTERN

Country and western music (also known as country music) grew out of folk music traditions in the southern United States. In the 20th century, it became hugely popular all around the world, and produced a number of superstars. Country and western songs are often based around simple chords, with words about love and romance.

Grand Ole Opry

In 1925, a radio station called WSM began broadcasting from Nashville. Three years later, it broadcast an evening of country and western music, which quickly became a weekly feature—this was the Grand Ole Opry. The success of the show drew country musicians to Nashville, and the city became a center for country and western music. Stars of the Grand Ole Opry included Roy Acuff and Hank Williams. In 1974, the show moved from a large church called the Ryman Auditorium to a new building at the center of a large amusement park called Opryland. The shows still continue today.

Dolly Parton (1946—)

Dolly Parton is one of country music's biggest stars. She was one of 12 children born into a poor farming family in Locust Ridge, Tennessee. By the age of 13 she was appearing at the Grand Ole Opry. She had her first hit in 1967, called "Dumb Blonde" and by the 1970s she had become a star of the country music scene. She moved into the pop world during the 1980s, also appearing in her first movie 9 to 5. She is a very talented singer and songwriter, with hits such as "Jolene" and "Tennessee Homesick Blues" to her name.

The Nashville Sound

For many years, shows from the Grand Ole Opry upheld traditional country values. For example, drums were not allowed on stage, only traditional country instruments such as the guitar, fiddle, banjo, or harmonica. But by the 1950s and 1960s many groups, including the Everly Brothers (right) and Gram Parsons, were producing records that blended country music with pop and rock sounds. This became known as the "Nashville Sound," and helped widen the appeal of the music.

Willie Nelson

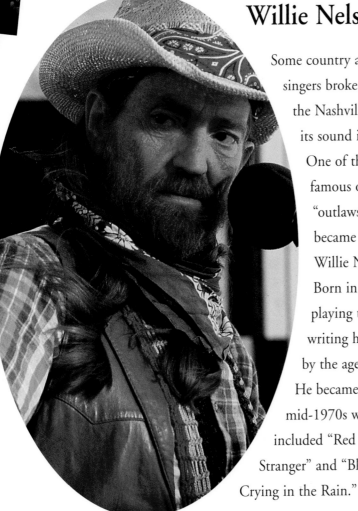

Some country and western singers broke away from the Nashville scene and its sound in the 1970s. One of the most famous of these "outlaws" as they became known was Willie Nelson (left). Born in Texas, he was playing the guitar and writing his own songs by the age of seven. He became a star in the mid-1970s with hits that included "Red Headed Stranger" and "Blue Eyes Crying in the Rain."

Country Tunes

1. *I Will Always Love You*
   Dolly Parton
2. *Stand By Your Man*
   Tammy Wynette
3. *Always On My Mind*
   Willie Nelson
4. *Coward Of The County*
   Kenny Rogers
5. *Hearts On Fire*
   Gram Parsons
6. *Rhinestone Cowboy*
   Glen Campbell
7. *Tearin' It Up*
   Garth Brooks
8. *Walls Of Time*
   Emmylou Harris
9. *Achy Breaky Heart*
   Billie Ray Cyrus
10. *I Walk The Line*
    Johnny Cash

• *See also pages 44-45, 94, 104*

DANCE

Since the beginning of time, the rhythms and sounds of music have fostered in people an irresistible urge to dance. We know from cave paintings that even prehistoric people danced. Every culture around the world has its own particular form of dance. Dancing for fun, for entertainment, in ritual, or to tell a story continues to be very important today.

Dance in Africa

This Shangaan dancer is performing a ritual dance in Zimbabwe, Africa. Dance is very important in African communities—events such as birth, death, and marriage are often marked by special dances. African dancers often paint their bodies, or wear elaborate masks. Dancing is also used to bring people in touch with the spirit world. In Zimbabwe these dances are often accompanied by an mbira, a thumb piano in which metal bars of different lengths are vibrated inside a resonating gourd.

Flamenco

Flamenco has its roots in the gypsy dances of southern Spain, and can be danced solo, or in groups. It can be performed to rhythmical clicking and singing, and is sometimes accompanied by guitars and castanets. The dancers' feet move with precision in complicated patterns, and the arms create flowing movements. Flamenco remains a vital part of Spanish life and culture. This flamenco dancer creates a blur of color, sound, and movement as she stamps and struts at a fair in Andalucia.

Dance in Southeast Asia

Classical dance in Southeast Asia is many centuries old. These dancers are performing in Cambodia, Southeast Asia. They are accompanied by a percussion orchestra, rather like a **gamelan** (see page 77). Expressions of the face and elaborate hand movements are used in these dances to tell a story, usually based on traditional folklore or legends.

• *See also pages 44, 49, 85*

DOUBLE BASS

The double bass was developed in the 16th century from the double bass viol, a flat-backed string instument played between the knees. It is the largest of the string instruments, and its deep sound provides the bass line for the classical orchestra.

Double Bass Group

As well as being a part of the classical orchestra, the double bass is also a key member of many jazz groups, where the deep, mellow sound of its strings being plucked (a technique called **pizzicato**) provides a steady bass line for the melodies above. It is used widely in ensemble playing as its unobtrusive sound complements almost any combination of instruments. Here, the double bass is being played alongside a violin, guitar, and tuba.

Playing the Double Bass

Double bass players often perch on a high stool to play their instrument, but it can also be played standing up. It has a very short spike, and stands just over six feet (2 meters) high. The shoulders of the double bass are dropped compared to the shape of the cello to make it easier for the player's left hand to reach the **strings**.

• See also pages 56, 57–59, 108–109

Drums are played all over the world. They are used in ceremonies and rituals, and for signaling and sending messages. Drums were traditionally used in battle, and are still used to set the pace for marching soldiers. The rhythms they produce are also an essential part of pop and rock music.

Rock Drums

The drums are an important instrument in rock. The drumming of Ringo Starr in the Beatles was a vital element of songs like "Taxman" and "Twist and Shout." Other notable rock drummers include Keith Moon from The Who and Charlie Watts from The Rolling Stones.

Slit Drums

Some drums are made by hollowing out a piece of wood or bamboo and making a slit along one side. They are called slit drums and are played by striking the drum with a beater, or with the hands.

Two-headed Drums

In many two-headed drums, the drum head is attached by lacing that runs from one end of the drum to the other. If the player squeezes the lacing, it stretches the skin on the drum head tighter. This makes the pitch of the drum higher. In this way, many different pitches can be played on the same drum. In West Africa, the kalangu is known as the "talking drum" because it can be used to imitate the different pitches of some languages in the region.

Frame Drums

A **frame drum** has a drum skin stretched over a thin, shallow frame. A tambourine is a kind of frame drum with jingles attached to the side. Frame drums have been particularly important to Native American, Arctic, and European folk communities. A type of frame drum called the bodhrán is used in Irish folk music. It is held in one hand, and played with a double-ended stick by the other hand.

• See also pages 39-40, 59, 60, 77-78, 91-93

From the very earliest times people have made music by clapping their hands, stamping their feet, and using their voices. Music has always been an important part of life in many traditions. The oldest musical instruments were fashioned out of whatever was close at hand—natural materials such as stones, hollow branches, and sea shells. More complicated instruments soon evolved out of these early efforts.

Music in China

Kneeling down, a female musician prepares to play her flute. This Chinese statuette comes from the period of the Tang Dynasty (A.D. 618–906) in China. It is one of several figures that were found in a tomb. In real life, this musician probably entertained the emperor and his courtiers at the imperial court. Music was very important in China from the earliest times. It was used for worship in the temples, and at festivals celebrating important events in the year such as planting crops and harvesting. Important instruments included the qin (a type of lute) and the sheng (a type of mouth organ made from bamboo pipes).

Ancient Greece

This Ancient Greek plate is about 2,500 years old, and depicts a woman playing a wind instrument with two pipes called an aulos. The aulos was a **reed** instrument belonging to the wind family with **finger holes** on both pipes. This instrument was hard to play. You can see that the player's cheeks are puffed out with the effort of blowing into the pipes. The aulos was an important instrument, used in Ancient Greek theatres to lead the chorus in Greek plays. It was also heard at ceremonies and feasts of all kinds.

Ancient Egypt

In Ancient Egyptian society, music was used in religious ceremonies and to entertain. This Ancient Egyptian tomb painting is about 3,500 years old. It comes from the tomb of a court official and shows two women—one playing a harp (right), the other playing a long-necked lute (left). The Egyptians also played various wind instruments including flutes, clarinets, oboes, and trumpets.

• See also pages 8, 48, 79-80

ELECTRONIC INSTRUMENTS

During the late 20th century several electronic instruments were developed, as inventors took advantage of new technology. Electronic instruments use electronic circuits to make the sound itself. Through sampling and synthesising, an infinite variety of sounds are placed at the fingertips of the performer.

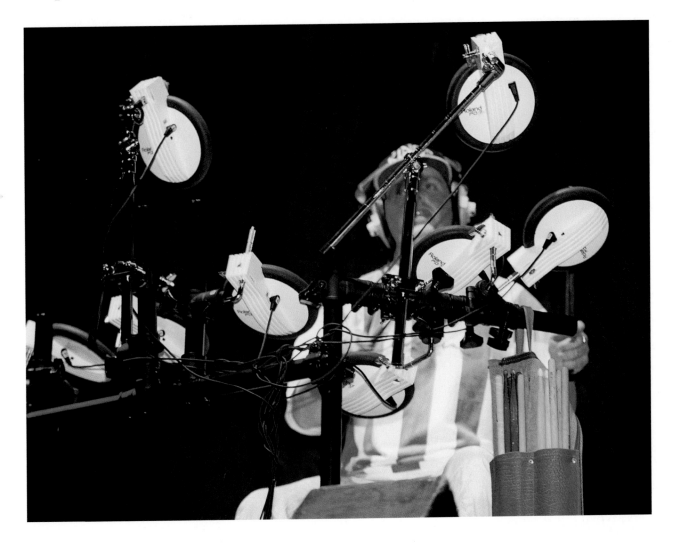

Electronic Drumkit

Today, many musicians use electronic rather than conventional drumkits. Electronic drumkits have pads that detect a drum-stick hitting it. Each hit triggers the synthesizer inside to make a sound. The pads are identical, but the synthesizer can be programed so that each of them sounds like a different size or type of drum.

The Drum Machine

Drum machines are music computers that can be used in the place of a drummer. They can be pre-programed with a series of different drum tracks. They are an invaluable part of many dance and hip-hop bands. Sounds are sampled from real drums and fed into the drum machine. The internal computer can then manipulate the sounds to produce an almost infinite variety of noises and rhythms.

The Synthesizer

Synthesizers produce a variety of sounds electronically, from the noise of a thunderstorm to that of the string section of a symphony orchestra. The first synthesizers were developed in the 1940s and started to become really popular in the 1960s. Many synthesizers have keyboards to control the sounds, but there are other versions such as synthesizer drums and synthesizer guitars.

• *See also pages 28, 56*

Music festivals are held all over the world and feature all types of music including classical, rock, pop, jazz, and folk. They are great social events, where people gather to hear live music and share in the experience with other fans. Festivals are often held in the summer months, when events can be held outdoors.

Woodstock

Woodstock was a famous three-day festival held in August 1969 in some fields near the small village of Woodstock, New York. It attracted hundreds of thousands of music fans who flocked to hear rock performers including Jefferson Airplane, Greatful Dead, Santana, The Who, Jimi Hendrix, and Janis Joplin. The festival quickly became part of rock legend.

On the Fringe

Besides the main shows of a festival, there are often lots of smaller events such as workshops and talks. These are known as "fringe" events. This picture was taken at an event on the beach in Aldeburgh, eastern England. Aldeburgh was the home of the British composer Benjamin Britten, who founded an annual festival in the town in 1948. These performers are dancing to Britten's "A Midsummer Night's Dream."

Opera Festivals

This dramatic stage set was part of a festival held in the Austrian city of Bregenz in 1999. It is a floating set for the **opera** "A Masked Ball" by the Italian composer Giuseppe Verdi. Festivals celebrating opera are held all over the world. Sometimes they are based around a single composer. The Bayreuth Opera Festival, for example, is held every year in the home town of the German composer Richard Wagner, and performers play only his music.

• See also pages 71-73

The flute is a high-pitched wind instrument with a beautiful, clear tone. The German inventor and flautist Thomas Boehm redesigned the flute in the 1840s, developing the pattern of **finger holes** and keys still in use today. The flute has a smaller cousin called the piccolo, which sounds one **octave** above the pitch of the flute.

Playing the Flute

The flute is played by blowing across the mouthhole. The air is directed from the lip of the hole into the pipe.

James Galway (1939–)

Most flutes are made from a mixture of nickel and silver, some from stainless steel. But the flautist James Galway has a very special flute made from gold. James Galway was born in Belfast, Northern Ireland and learned to play the penny whistle as a child. He went on to study the flute in London and Paris before becoming an orchestral flautist. In 1969 he became Principal (first) flute in the Berlin Philharmonic Orchestra. He has had a successful solo career, becoming famous for the warm tone he produces.

FOLK MUSIC

Folk music is a form of oral history, telling the story of a community or people through song. Different regions and communities around the world often have their own traditional songs and **melodies**, which have been handed down through the generations. Work songs such as **sea shanties** are examples of folk music, as are ballads that tell a story. Folk music can also be political—singers such as Bob Dylan have used the format to protest against political injustices.

Folk Dancing

A lot of folk music is used as an accompaniment to dancing. This picture shows a traditional type of dance seen in England, called morris dancing. Morris dances are often accompanied by the accordion, and morris dancers often wear bells on their legs that jingle as they move. Tunes for dancing often have a strong beat, such as the rhythmic sounds of Spanish flamenco dancing.

Collecting Folk Music

This man is playing a hardanger fiddle, a traditional Norwegian folk fiddle. This fiddle was mainly used to play dance tunes. The Norwegian composer Edvard Grieg knew many of the traditional tunes of his homeland and used them in some of his music. He was not the only composer to be interested in folk music. In the 20th century, composers such as Englishman Ralph Vaughan Williams, and the Hungarians Zoltan Kodaly and Bela Bartok toured their countries, writing down and recording folk tunes before they were lost. The American composer Aaron Copland also used folk tunes in much of his music.

Bob Dylan (1941–)

Bob Dylan was born in Duluth, Minnesota. His family name is Robert Allen Zimmerman, but he called himself Bob Dylan after the poet Dylan Thomas. Dylan learned to play guitar and harmonica as a child, and was inspired by the music of Hank Williams and Woody Guthrie. In 1961, he moved to New York where he released an album of original songs called "The Freewheelin' Bob Dylan," which included the protest song "Blowin' In The Wind." Bob Dylan soon became a well-known name in the world of folk music, but in 1965 he shocked the folk audience at the Newport Folk Festival by playing with an electric guitar. His first pop hit was "Like A Rolling Stone" in 1967. Dylan has continued to write and tour, returning to his folk roots in the 1990s with the albums "Good As I Been To You," and "World Gone Wrong."

Protest Music

In the 1950s and 60s, there was a revival of interest in folk music in the United States. At first singers drew on traditional folk tunes and words, but songwriters such as Woody Guthrie soon began to compose new songs in a folk style. Like many traditional folk songs, these new songs often had a political message, and they were known as "protest songs." The singer-songwriter Pete Seeger wrote many protest songs including "Where Have All The Flowers Gone." The group Peter, Paul and Mary, shown on this album cover, had a hit with one of Seeger's songs, "If I Had A Hammer."

• See also pages 30-31, 41, 112

GUITAR

The guitar is a plucked string instrument, popular all over the world. Its popularity comes from the fact that it is easily carried and can be played as a solo instrument, to accompany singing or dancing, or to accompany other instruments. The guitar originally came from Spain, but became well-known across Europe during the 17th century.

Jumbo Guitar

This huge guitar is being played in a folk group at Teotihuacan, Mexico. Guitars became popular in areas colonized by Spanish settlers in the 16th and 17th centuries. Today, folk guitars of all sizes are found in Central and South America. Some have the usual six **strings**; others have twelve strings tuned in pairs.

Playing the Guitar

The design of the guitar has changed very little since the 17th century. The body is a fat, figure eight shape. There are six strings, tuned to the notes E, A, D, G, B, and high E. On the **fingerboard** there are metal ridges, called **frets**, which indicate to players where to place their fingers. The frets also raise the stopped string slightly above the fingerboard, allowing it to vibrate and sound clearly.

The Electric Guitar

The electric guitar is a key part of nearly every modern pop and rock band, adding a powerful and exciting backing to vocals. Musicians such as Jimi Hendrix and Eric Clapton are masters of the instrument. In an electric guitar, the sound is still produced by the vibration of the string, but it is amplified and often modified using electric pick-ups.

Jimi Hendrix (1942–1970)

Jimi Hendrix, born in Seattle, Washington in 1942, was one of the greatest electric guitarists of all time. Hendrix learned to play the guitar as a teenager. In 1966, he went to London and formed his own group, the Jimi Hendrix Experience. His playing, invention, and showmanship were soon making an impression and the band had its first Top Ten hit in 1967 with "Hey Joe." In the same year, the band played for the first time in the United States at the Monterey Pop Festival. Sadly, Hendrix's career was tragically cut short—he died in London at age 28.

At the Ball

These costumed players are attending a ball, given in Spain in 1629. They are each playing a vihuela, an early relation of the guitar. The vihuela was a Spanish instrument popular during the Renaissance period. The guitar started to take over from its earlier relations, such as the vihuela and the lute, during the 17th century. The baroque guitar had only five strings, the sixth string was added in the 1790s.

• *See also pages 33, 93-94*

HARP

The harp is a romantic stringed instrument that has a separate string for every pitch. When plucked, they generate a sound like rippling water. The harp became an important member of the classical orchestra during the Romantic period, when composers such as Hector Berlioz and Peter Tchaikovsky began to write pieces specifically for the harp.

Playing the Strings

There are 47 strings on an orchestral harp. Some of them are colored, to help the harpist—all the C strings are red and all the F strings are blue. The harpist can pluck the strings on their own, or in chords. The harpist's hands can also be run fast across the strings to produce a beautiful shimmering effect called a **glissando**.

Raising the Pitch

Modern orchestral harps have seven pedals. Pressing one of these pedals half-way raises the pitch of the strings by a semitone. Pressing it down all the way raises the pitch by a tone. This means that every string on the harp can sound three different notes. The harpist's left foot operates the pedals for the pitches D, C, and B; the right foot operates the pedals for E, F, G, and A.

• See also pages 8, 38, 83, 106

Hip-hop grew out of the reggae tradition of talking in rhythm over a musical backing. Rapping combines with breakbeats and music samples to create fresh new sounds. The music is particularly innovative in the inner cities of New York and Los Angeles. A whole culture has grown up around hip-hop music, including breakdancing and graffiti art.

Grandmaster Flash

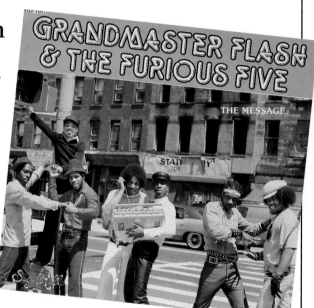

Grandmaster Flash was born in the Bronx district of New York, and began working as a D.J. in his teens. He developed many of the **scratching** techniques that became an important part of hip-hop. Scratching is the term for moving the needle on records by hand to create special effects. Grandmaster Flash was skilled at effects such as moving precisely between tracks, and repeating short sections of music. He teamed up with other rappers called the Furious Five. They had their biggest hit in 1982 with "The Message."

Breakdancing

One of the features of hip-hop is a type of dance known as breakdancing, which became popular during the late 1980s and early 1990s. This dancing involved high-energy spins and was a form of street dancing which moved into the nightclubs. Michael Jackson made use of street breakdancers in videos such as "Billie Jean" and "Beat It."

Coolio (1962–)

Born in the tough Compton district of Los Angeles, Coolio's real name is Artis Ivey. He specializes in reality-based rhymes, without the violence of contemporaries such as Ice Cube and Dr. Dre. His debut release, "Whacha Gonna Do?" was one of Los Angeles' first rap records, and he launched his career performing shows for the legendary rap radio station K.D.A.Y./Los Angeles. After 2 years as a firefighter, he returned to music, joining the hip-hop group WC And The MADD Circle, but he enjoyed his greatest success as a solo artist. The song "Gangsta's Paradise," propelled him into worldwide stardom. Tours with R. Kelly and a film career have all helped to raise his profile still further.

Hip-Hop and Rap Tunes

1. **The Message**
     Grandmaster Flash &
     The Furious Five
2. **Parents Just Don't Understand**
     DJ Jazzy Jeff &
     The Fresh Prince
3. **Rapper's Delight**
     Sugerhill Gang
4. **Ms. Jackson**
     Outkast
5. **Scenario**
     Tribe Called Quest
6. **Me Myself and I**
     De La Soul
7. **It's Tricky**
     Run D.M.C.
8. **Waterfalls**
     T.L.C.
9. **Fly Girl**
     Queen Latifa
10. **Doo Wop [That Thing]**
     Lauryn Hill

Graffiti Art

The culture of hip-hop includes music, dance, and art. Graffiti art has become an important part of the hip-hop movement. This colorful spray-painted art now appears in many cities around the world.

• See also page 103

The modern orchestral horn, known as the French horn, is related to the old metal horns traditionally used to herald the start of a hunt. Its warming sound adds color and depth to both orchestras and brass bands. In the early 19th century, **valves** were added to make it easier for players to sound different **pitches**. Previously, players removed and inserted lengths of tubing called crooks to alter the sound produced.

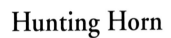

Hunting Horn

This beautiful carved horn dates from the 1500s. It is made from elephant ivory, and horns like this were known as oliphants (elephants). It is probable that they were not actually used for hunting, but kept as prized possessions by wealthy noblemen. Horns used for hunting were usually made from the horns of rams or from metal.

Playing the French Horn

These musicians are playing double horns in F and B flat—the most common type of French horn found in the classical orchestra. These French horns are known as double horns because they have a valve that changes the pitch of the instrument from F to B♭. The right hand is inserted inside the bell of the horn. This not only helps to support the horn, but the hand position inside the bell can also be used to alter the sound. The left hand operates the valves which change the pitch of the note.

• See also pages 9, 16-17, 20, 76, 91

IMPROVISATION

Improvisation is the art of performing music spontaneously without reading from written music. Improvisation is very important in many types of jazz music. In the past, many famous classical composers were also renowned for their ability to make up music on the spot.

Early Improvisers

Many people think that jazz is the only type of music that makes use of improvisation. But classical composers such as Bach, Mozart, and Beethoven were all famous in their own time for their improvisations. Sadly, this spontaneous music was never written down, and as there were no methods of recording music, we have no record of exactly what these improvisations sounded like. Today, some organists continue to specialize in improvisation.

Trumpet Improvisations

Louis Armstrong was responsible for the earliest true improvisation in jazz music. He improvised on his trumpet (shown here on the right), shortening and lengthening notes, and changing the rhythm. Soon, he was improvising dazzling variations on **melodies** and making up spontaneous melodies. His recordings "Potato Head Blues" and "West End Blues" with his band the Hot Five were influential for all jazz musicians.

52

● *See also pages 14-15, 53-55, 96, 102*

The story of jazz began in the late 19th century in America. Jazz grew out of a wide variety of influences, but particularly the music of African-Americans who were determined to keep their own traditions alive even during the time of slavery. Other important influences in the history of jazz included European **harmonies** and American band instruments.

Jazz Vocalists

Ella Fitzgerald was one of the best-known and accomplished jazz singers of all time. Her first hit, "A Tisket A Tasket" was recorded in 1938. She was famous for her "scat" singing—improvising rhythmic lines to nonsense syllables such as "doo" or "da." Other famous female jazz vocalists included Sarah Vaughn, Billie Holiday, and Nina Simone. Male vocalists included Louis Armstrong, who invented scat singing, and Fats Waller, who wrote witty words to his songs, which he accompanied on the piano.

The Cotton Club

The Cotton Club was one of the main centers of jazz in New York City during the 1920s, featuring artists such as Duke Ellington and his band. The 1920s is often called the "jazz age," as the craze for jazz music spread across the United States. Although jazz originally developed in southern cities such as New Orleans, many jazz musicians moved to cities in the north, notably Chicago and New York. Live jazz was broadcast on radio stations across the country, and jazz recordings sold well to an eager public.

● *See also pages 14, 23, 34, 52, 56, 96, 99, 100, 102, 109*

Miles Davis (1926–1991)

*M*iles Davis was born in Alton, Illinois. At the age of 19 he went to New York to study at the Juilliard School, but he was more interested in jazz than classical music, and he began to play regularly with saxophonist Charlie Parker. However, Davis soon developed his own style of slow, moody jazz, known as "cool jazz." Later in his career, Davis experimented with mixing jazz and rock music, creating an exciting new sound called "fusion" jazz.

Ragtime

Scott Joplin, shown here on this postage stamp, was the most famous player of an important early type of jazz—ragtime. This kind of jazz was played mainly on the piano. It gets its name from the "ragged time" or syncopation of the music. This means that a strong, regular four-beat **rhythm** played by the left hand is set against jagged rhythms that fall against the main beats in the right hand. Ragtime was very popular in the 1890s and early 20th century, and it was an important influence on later types of jazz.

Jazz Tunes

1. *Maple Leaf Drag*
   Scott Joplin
2. *The Hot Fives and Sevens*
   Louis Armstrong
3. *Carnegie Hall Concert*
   Duke Ellington
4. *Ain't Misbehavin'*
   Fats Waller
5. *The Savoy Recordings*
   Charlie Parker
6. *Kind of Blue*
   Miles Davis
7. *Lady in Satin*
   Billie Holiday
8. *A Tisket, A Tasket*
   Ella Fitzgerald
9. *Giant Steps*
   John Coltrane
10. *Koln Concert*
    Keith Jarrett

Dizzy Gillespie and Bebop

The trumpeter Dizzy Gillespie and the saxophonist Charlie Parker (see page 98) were known for developing a new style of jazz known as **bebop**. Bebop became popular in the 1940s. relied on complicated, virtuoso solos from the main sts in a group. This cartoon of Dizzy Gillespie shows playing his trumpet with the bell pointing upwards than straight in front. The story goes that someone fell his trumpet and bent it, whereupon Gillespie decided that he red the sound that way anyway!

• See also pages 96, 99, 100, 102

55

KEYBOARD INSTRUMENTS

Keyboard instruments are used in almost every genre of music today. The piano is used in classical, jazz, and pop music, the organ in religious music, while the harpsichord is used in some chamber groups. The development of electric keyboards and synthesizers have extended the possibilities of these instruments still further.

The Organ

This ornate organ is in Tokyo's concert hall, Geijutsu Gekijo. The organ is both a wind and keyboard instrument, because it uses air forced through pipes to sound notes played on a keyboard. In previous centuries, the air was usually provided by someone pumping a bellows at the side of the organ. In modern organs, the air is generated by an electric motor. The keyboard is called a manual, and many organs have more than one, as well as a keyboard for the feet, called the pedalboard. When the player presses a note, levers operate to allow air to flow through a particular pipe, sounding the note. The organ is capable of producing many different sounds.

Harpsichord

The harpsichord may look like a piano, but its sound is quite different. Unlike the piano, where the **strings** are hit with a hammer, the strings of a harpsichord are plucked, giving a bright, delicate tone. The harpsichord became very important in the 17th and 18th centuries, both as a solo instrument and in instrumental groups.

The Liszt Fan Club

This 19th-century cartoon shows the composer and virtuoso piano player, Franz Liszt, giving a concert before an audience of hysterical women. Liszt's genius on the piano, as well as his looks and passionate character, won him many admirers across Europe—much like a pop star in the 21st century. This Hungarian composer wrote a huge amount of music for the piano, often rewriting orchestral works for the keyboard. Liszt was the first performer to popularize complete concerts of solo piano music.

Keyboard Tunes

1. *Piano Concertos*
   W. A. Mozart
2. *Piano Sonatas*
   L. van Beethoven
3. *Mazurkas*
   Chopin
4. *Prelude and Fugues*
   J.S. Bach
5. *Mephisto Waltz*
   Liszt
6. *Piano Concerto (Op. 83)*
   Brahms
7. *Twenty-four Preludes*
   Debussy
8. *Gymnopedies*
   Satie
9. *Piano Concerto*
   Gershwin
10. *Four Interludes*
    John Cage

Piano

The piano is capable of producing a far greater variety of sounds and a wider range of volume than the harpsichord. The player can vary the sound produced by pressing a **key** gently to play a soft note, or pressing a key more vigorously to play a louder note. Large grand pianos for concert halls can measure up to nine feet (3 meters) long and weigh up to 900 lb (408 kg). The piano lid is opened for concerts, as it helps to project the sound of the piano towards the audience.

Elton John (1947–)

The piano is also an important pop and rock instrument, used by performers such as Elton John. Born Reginald Dwight, John began playing the piano at the age of four, and won a scholarship to the Royal Academy in London when he was eleven. His piano playing is a feature of most of his hits. He joined his first band, Bluesology, in 1961, but left at the end of the 1960s in search of solo success. He teamed up with lyricist Bernie Taupin at the record label DJM in 1968, and the duo went on to have a string of hits, including "Your Song," "Rocket Man," and "Candle In The Wind." In 1997, John re-released "Candle In The Wind" with new lyrics to commemorate the death of Diana, Princess of Wales. The single occupied the top spot in the United States for 13 weeks.

• *See also pages 20, 29, 40*

MARCHING BANDS

Music is used to add spirit and drama to parades and festivals around the world. In the United States and parts of Europe, the music is usually provided by spectacular marching bands. Marching bands are made up of instruments that can be played on the move, including brass and woodwind instruments, drums, and other percussion instruments that provide the beat for marching.

The Sousaphone

This man is playing a sousaphone. This instrument was named in honor of the American bandmaster John Philip Sousa, who suggested that the instrument be made. It is a type of tuba that can be played sitting down or while marching This is achieved by resting the instrument on the left shoulder. The bell is detachable and can point forwards or backwards. Today, many sousaphones are made with fiberglass bells to reduce their weight.

Columbus Day Parade

Columbus Day is a national holiday across the United States, and in several countries in Central and South America. It is usually held on the second Monday in October and it celebrates the arrival of Christopher Columbus on American soil in 1492. Dazzling parades such as this are held all across the country.

Sousa's band

This collection of music, published in Germany, contains some of John Philip Sousa's most famous marches. Sousa was an American composer as well as a bandmaster. He formed his band in 1892, and wrote many marches for it, earning his nickname the "March King." Some of his most famous marches include "The Stars and Stripes Forever," "The Liberty Bell March," and "Manhattan Beach."

Military Bands

Military bands were originally made up of the instruments used by ancient armies for sending signals and encouraging the troops. Today, they usually include instruments such as piccolos, clarinets, saxophones, cornets, trombones, cymbals, and drums. This military band is performing in the Crystal Palace in London, in 1854.

• See also pages 78, 84, 109

MELODY AND HARMONY

A melody is comprised of a series of notes of different **pitches** and **rhythms**. If you add a complementary line of melody to your original, you have **harmony**. Harmony is used in all types of music, from classical compositions to pop music performed by acts such as the Backstreet Boys.

Writing a Tune

In a melody, the notes can move step by step, or in jumps skipping notes in-between. The best tunes are often very simple. A well-known melody such as "Three Blind Mice" has just two main sections, with the first section repeated at the end of the tune. When you try writing your own melodies, remember that you can do a lot with just one simple musical idea. Try varying it, turning it upside-down, or writing it backwards and see what happens!

Chords

When you sound two or more notes together, for example on the piano or guitar, you are playing a **chord**. Chords are often used to provide the accompaniment for a melody. Some chords sound more pleasing to the ear than others. A **triad** is a chord with three notes: the main note at the bottom called the root, a note a third above the root; and a note a fifth above the root; Triads can be built on any note of the scale. They provide the building blocks for harmony in classical music.

Counterpoint

Not all melody is accompanied by chords. Early composers wove a second melody above or below the first to create a kind of music called **counterpoint**. *In counterpoint, two or more lines of music are played or sung at the same time as each other. If you have ever sung a round, such as "Row, Row, Row Your Boat," then you have sung a piece written in counterpoint.*

• *See also pages 21, 52, 53, 84*

MOTOWN

otown was the name of an independent record label that started up in Detroit, in the Midwest, in 1959. Its artists included the Supremes, the Four Tops, and individual stars like Al Green and Marvin Gaye. The name Motown was short for "motor town" because Detroit was famous for its motor industry. The man responsible for the Motown sound was Berry Gordy Jr., the head of the record company.

Stevie Wonder (1950–)

Stevie Wonder was a child prodigy who began a recording career at the age of just eleven, despite going blind five years earlier. His recordings were infectious bundles of vinyl energy, and within a few years he become Motown's number one star. Unusually among performers of the era, he wrote most of his own material. Famous hits included "Fingertips (Part 2)," "My Cherie Amour," and "Masterblaster." Albums such as "Songs in the Key of Life" and "Music of My Mind" remain true classics to this day.

The First Girl Band?

The Supremes were one of the most popular groups on the Motown label. They were the most successful black group of the 1960s, scoring five Number One hits in a row. The group had slimmed down from a quartet to the trio of Diana Ross, Mary Wilson, and Florence Ballard by 1961. Hits included "Where Did Our Love Go?," "Baby Love," and "Come See About Me." Ross (left) was to become increasingly prominent in the group, and in 1967, the band was renamed "Diana Ross and The Supremes." In 1969, Ross embarked on a solo career.

• See also page 85

Motown Maestro

Smoky Robinson (seated) has made a name for himself as one of the greatest composers and singers of romantic soul music. His beautifully expressive high tenor is instantly recognizable. He entered the music world in the 1960s with his band The Miracles, releasing smash hits such as "I Second That Emotion" and "The Tracks Of My Tears" on the Motown label. Dubbed "America's greatest living poet" by Bob Dylan, Robinson was also making a name for himself as a songwriter and lyricist, penning the worldwide hit "My Girl" for The Temptations. Robinson went on to have a highly successful solo career. His biggest individual hit was probably "Being With You."

Marvin Gaye (1939–1984)

Born in Washington, D.C., Marvin was the son of a minister who worked for the conservative "House of God" religious sect. His childhood was harsh, peppered with beatings and rows. Gaye found respite in the church choir, where he began performing at the age of three. He started working for Motown as a session drummer, but soon began recording as a vocalist.
His hits included "How Sweet It Is (To Be Loved By You)," "Ain't No Mountain High Enough," and the landmark album "What's Going On." This masterpiece explored political issues such as poverty, race, and the Vietnam war. Gaye's career was cut short in 1984, when he was shot and killed.

MOVIE SOUNDTRACKS

When you go to watch a movie you are surrounded by the sound of the film—the actors' voices, special sound effects, and the music. The music of a film is called its soundtrack and is extremely important for creating the right atmosphere. This is why film directors spend a lot of time and money getting exactly the right composers and music for their movie soundtracks.

John Williams's Films

One of the best known of all film score composers is the American John Williams. He was the son of a musician who worked in a movie studio, and he studied at the Julliard School in New York. His name has become particularly associated with the movie directors George Lucas and Steven Spielberg. He wrote the music for the *Star Wars* films, as well as blockbusters such as *E.T.*, *Jaws*, *Raiders of the Lost Ark*, and *Saving Private Ryan*. In his long career, he has won six Oscars.

Michael Nyman (1944–)

*B*orn in Britain, Michael Nyman studied at the Royal Academy of Music in London. He was influenced by experimental composers such as the Americans John Cage, Steve Reich, and Philip Glass. In 1977 he formed a band that was to become the Michael Nyman Band. In the early 1980s he began to work with the movie director Peter Greenaway, writing the music for a film called The Draughtsman's Contract. *He has continued to write film scores, including the music for* The Piano.

• See also pages 86-87

Henry V

Laurence Olivier's classic film version of William Shakespeare's play *Henry V* features music by the British composer William Walton. This was Walton's first film score, but it was a huge success. It made use of Elizabethan-style music, appropriate to the period of the film, as well as more modern and Romantic sounds. Walton went on to write film music for many other movies including *As You Like It*, *The Battle of Britain*, and *Richard III*.

Making a Recording

The film score is usually one of the last elements to be added to the soundtrack of a movie. Sometimes a movie makes use of well-known pieces of music or songs, but most movies have music written specially for them. The director and the composer watch a rough edit of the film and discuss what type of music is needed. The composer then writes the music, and it is specially recorded in a studio. This picture shows the composer John Barry at a recording session for the James Bond film *Live and Let Die*.

MUSICALS

Musicals developed in the United States out of operetta and **music hall** at the beginning of the 20th century. Musicals blend popular song and spoken words with spectacular dance routines. Famous musical composers include Jerome Kern, Irving Berlin, Cole Porter, Richard Rodgers and Oscar Hammerstein, Leonard Bernstein, Stephen Sondheim, and Andrew Lloyd Webber. Hit musicals include *Cats*, *West Side Story*, and *The Lion King*.

West Side Story

This scene comes from Leonard Bernstein's musical *West Side Story*. Bernstein wrote the music, and Stephen Sondheim wrote the lyrics (words). The book of the musical is based on William Shakespeare's play *Romeo and Juliet*, but set in 1950s New York. Bernstein used snappy Latin American **rhythms** in his music to portray the Puerto Rican community from which Maria, the heroine comes. Famous songs from *West Side Story* including "Maria" and "Tonight."

Oklahoma!

The names Rodgers and Hammerstein have become linked together because of their string of hit musicals that included *Oklahoma!*, *South Pacific*, *The King and I*, and *The Sound of Music*. This picture shows a scene from *Oklahoma!* It was first staged in 1943 on Broadway, and was an immediate success. It included a ballet, based on American square dancing, as well as wonderful songs and a gripping storyline.

Andrew Lloyd Webber

Cats is just one of the many musicals written by the British composer Andrew Lloyd Webber. Lloyd Webber has a string of hits dating back to the 1970s, which succeeded both in Britain and in the United States. They include *Jesus Christ Superstar, Evita, Phantom of the Opera,* and *Starlight Express.* Lloyd Webber's musicals make use of elaborate stage settings and special effects. His musicals have also produced many hit songs, including "Don't Cry For Me Argentina," from the musical *Evita.*

Show Boat

Show Boat was a milestone in the development of the musical, because it made the songs and dance routines central to the story and dealt with some serious issues, including racial discrimination. When it opened in 1927, it was a huge hit on Broadway in New York. Another famous song that comes from *Show Boat* is "Can't Help Lovin' That Man." Here Paul Robeson sings the song "Ol' Man River" in a 1936 production of the musical.

The Musical That
Touched a Generation

CATS ™

NOW AND FOREVER

• *See also page 99*

NOTATION

In ancient times, music was not written down. People learned tunes and ways of playing instruments, and passed these traditions down from generation to generation. It was not until medieval times in Europe that monks started to experiment with writing symbols down on paper to help them remember music. Writing music down is called **notation**.

Ancient Chinese Notation

The European system of notation has become the best-known method of writing music down. But different methods of notation were developed in places such as ancient China and India. These Chinese symbols are the notation for a piece called "Hymn of the Temple of the Unborn."

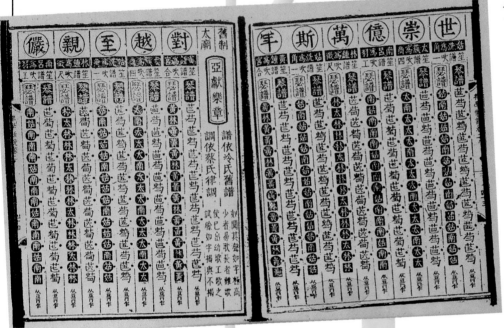

Writing Music Down

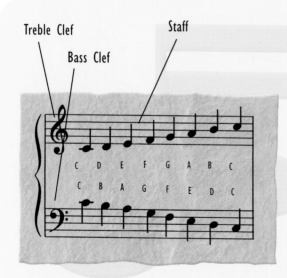

Treble Clef
Bass Clef
Staff

Musical **notes** are written down using five lines, called the **staff**. Each line and each space represents a note of different **pitch**. The higher the note on the staff, the higher its pitch. The notes are given letter names using the first seven letters of the alphabet: A, B, C, D, E, F, and G. The sign at the beginning of the staff is called a clef. This fixes the pitch of one of the lines of the staff. The most common clefs are the treble and bass clefs. The treble clef fixes the second line up as the note G. The bass clef fixes the second line down as the note F.

Psalms

In medieval times, monks and nuns memorized the chants that they sang every day in abbeys and monasteries. But this was a long and difficult task, and some monks began to try and write the chants down. This picture shows a chant written on a four-line staff (the red lines), indicating the pitch of the notes. The length of different notes is shown by their shape. The words of the chant are written beneath the staff.

A Love Song

Early composers wrote down their compositions in a number of creative ways. This 14th century love song, "Belle, bonne," was written down by the French composer Baude Cordier in the shape of a heart. This staff has five lines, just like the one we use to write music down today.

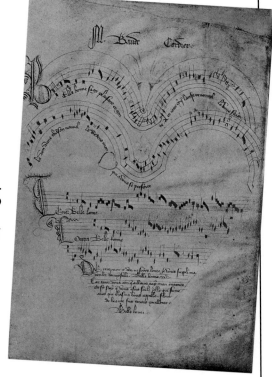

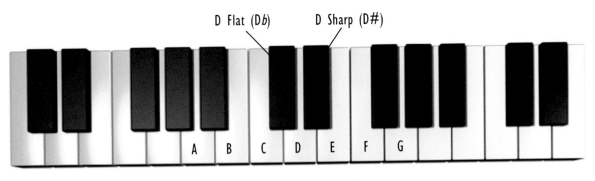

Sharps and Flats

If you look at the piano keyboard, you will see that it has black as well as white keys. The white keys are named A, B, C, D, E, F, and G. The black notes take their names from neighboring white notes. When writing music, if you want to indicate the black note a **semitone** (half a tone) above D, you write a **sharp** sign after the D (D#).

If you want to indicate the black note a semitone below D you write a **flat** after the note (D*b*).

• *See also page 90*

OBOE

The oboe is a relative of an early instrument called the shawm. Shawms were double-**reed** instruments that produced a loud sound, suitable for outdoor music. The oboe was developed during the 17th century for playing indoors. It is an important member of the classical orchestra and many chamber groups.

Mouthpiece

The orchestral oboe has a double reed made from two thin pieces of reed. The player puts the reed between the lips and blows, making the reed vibrate. This is what gives the oboe its characteristic tone. Oboes are about 24 inches (60 cm) long, and are made in three sections, usually out of wood. The oboe is the instrument to which the rest of the orchestra tunes. Before the start of a rehearsal or a concert, the oboe player sounds an A. The other musicians then tune their instruments accordingly.

Oboe Relations

The oboe (shown right) has two larger relations. The *oboe d'amore* ("oboe of love") is slightly longer than the oboe and has a rounded bottom. It makes a beautiful, plaintive sound and it was a favorite instrument of the 17th-century composer J.S. Bach. The *cor anglais* ("English horn") is longer, with a much deeper sound than the oboe. It, too, has a rounded end which makes the lower **notes** sound richer.

• See also pages 20, 38, 79, 116

Opera is one of the most passionate of musical art forms. Stories of love and tragedy are told on stage like a play, but the characters sing, rather than speak their words, to the accompaniment of an orchestra. Opera began in Italy in the early 1600s. The operas of one the first opera composers, the Italian Claudio Monteverdi, are still performed today.

Speaking and Singing

This colorful stage setting is from a performance of *Princess Ida*, an operetta written by Gilbert and Sullivan. An **operetta** is a light-hearted opera, with spoken words as well as singing. Another famous example is *Die Fledermaus* (*The Bat*) by the Viennese waltz-composer, Johann Strauss the Younger. W.S. Gilbert and Arthur Sullivan became a celebrated pair in the late 19th century when they produced a series of operettas that were all huge hits, including *The Pirates of Penzance* and *The Mikado*.

Opera Tunes

1. *Orfeo*
   Claudio Monteverdi
2. *Dido and Aeneas*
   Henry Purcell
3. *The Magic Flute*
   W.A. Mozart
4. *The Barber of Seville*
   G. Rossini
5. *Rigoletto*
   G. Verdi
6. *The Bartered Bride*
   B. Smetana
7. *La Bohème*
   G. Puccini
8. *Porgy and Bess*
   G. Gershwin
9. *Let's Make an Opera*
   B. Britten
10. *Nixon in China*
    J. Adams

The Magic Flute

This dramatic set is for a performance of Mozart's **opera** *The Magic Flute*. The opera was first performed in 1791. This set was designed for an 1816 performance. *The Magic Flute* features some of Mozart's best-loved characters, including the Queen of the Night, the bird-catcher Papageno and his partner Papagena. The story revolves around a handsome young man called Tamino who has to undergo a series of trials to win the love of the Queen of the Night's beautiful daughter.

Puccini's Greatest Hits

The Italian composer Giacomo Puccini wrote some of the most successful operas of all time. Inspired by Verdi, Puccini decided as a young man that he wanted to write operas. His earliest successful opera, *Manon Lescaut*, was first performed in 1893. He went on to produce a string of hits such as *La Bohème*, *Tosca*, and *Madame Butterfly*. In all of these operas, the heroine of the piece dies tragically at the end.

Giuseppe Verdi (1813–1901)

Verdi was born in the north of Italy in 1813. He studied music and became determined to see one of his operas performed at La Scala, the famous opera house in Milan. His first success was with Nabucco *in 1842. He followed this with a stream of thirteen operas in just eight years—some more successful than others. In the 1850s, he composed the operas for which he is known today,* Rigoletto, Il Trovatore *and* La Traviata. *Later in his life, Verdi became involved in politics, becoming a figurehead for the movement to unite Italy during civil unrest. He was elected as a member of the new Italian parliament in 1874.*

Opera in China

Opera has been performed in China for several centuries. At the court of the emperor, elaborate operas were performed with singing and dancing. They were often based on Chinese folk stories and legends. There was also opera for the ordinary people, with acrobatics and mime, as well as puppet operas. Today, singers in Chinese opera are accompanied by bowed and plucked lutes, flutes, and a drum with a sharp sound to keep time. Pictured here is a member of the Peking Opera performing a role from "*Wild Boar Forest.*"

Porgy and Bess

One of the best-known operas of the 20th century is *Porgy and Bess* by the American composer George Gershwin. Gershwin is famous for his popular jazz songs such as "Fascinatin' Rhythm" and "Lady be Good." But in this opera he mixed classical and jazz styles very successfully. The story, based on a novel by Du Bose Heyward, is set in New Orleans and tells the story of an African-American community. The opera contains several songs which have become hits in their own right, including "Summertime" and "It Ain't Necessarily So."

• *See also pages 20, 25, 26, 42, 100, 112*

ORCHESTRA

Orchestras vary greatly around the world. In Southeast Asia, they are made up almost entirely of percussion instruments, while the classical **symphony** orchestra is made up of different sections including **strings**, woodwind, brass, and percussion. Today there are classical symphony orchestras in most of the world's major cities.

The Conductor

The charismatic American composer and conductor Leonard Bernstein (see page 66) is shown here during a performance at the Carnegie Hall in New York. Like Bernstein, many conductors use a short white stick, called a baton, to make their beating easier to see. As well as beating time, the conductor is in charge of the interpretation of the music—how fast or slow it should go, how loud or soft it should be played. Early orchestras did not have a separate conductor—instead they were led by the first violinist, or by a soloist from the keyboard. But in the 19th century, as orchestras became bigger and the music more complex, the first professional conductors emerged.

Hector Berlioz (1803–69)

This 19th-century painting depicts the French composer Hector Berlioz and his orchestra. Berlioz started a career in medicine, but in 1826 he left medical school and went to the Music Consevatoire in Paris. A year later he went to the theatre to see a performance of Hamlet. There he fell in love with an English actress called Harriet Smithson—a passion that was to last for many years. He composed his orchestral work "Fantastic Symphony" in 1830, based on "Episodes in the Life of an Artist." He became famous for using huge orchestras, and often conducted his own works.

The Gamelan Orchestra

The **gamelan** orchestra is found in Java, Bali, and Lombok, islands of Indonesia. Large orchestras can be made up of up to 40 players. There is no conductor, but a central drummer leads the whole **ensemble**. The gamelan includes two types of metal xylophone called saron and gender (at the front of the picture), kettle gongs (at the back left of the picture), gongs, and drums. The most sacred instrument in the whole gamelan is the gong ageng, a large hanging gong made from bronze. It is played at the beginning and end of every piece.

The Symphony Orchestra

The modern **symphony** orchestra is usually made up of about 100 instruments, although this changes depending upon the kind of music being played. For a classical piece such as a symphony by Haydn or Mozart, the number is reduced to suit the smaller scale of the music. However, pieces by composers such as Gustav Mahler, Richard Strauss, or Hector Berlioz call for a huge orchestra, often with added instruments. For example, in his "Symphony of a Thousand" (8th Symphony), Mahler writes for five clarinets instead of the usual two, and eight French horns instead of the usual four, as well as a range of unusual instruments.

• See also pages 16, 23, 51, 77, 78, 106, 114, 116

The percussion family includes virtually anything that produces a sound when struck or shaken. Some of the basic instruments of the percussion section of the classical orchestra include the timpani or kettledrums, cymbals, triangle, sidedrum, bass drum, xylophone, and **glockenspiel**. But depending on what piece of music is being played, an almost infinite number of other instruments can be added.

Dancing Jingles

Many percussion instruments sound when they are shaken, meaning that they can easily be combined with dance. They mirror in sound the movements of the body. Indian dancers wear rows of bells around their ankles and waists that jingle as they move. Jingles can be made from metal, like these bells, or sometimes from shells or nuts.

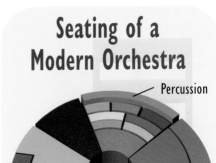

Seating of a Modern Orchestra

Percussion

The percussion section is usually at the back of the orchestra, behind the brass.

Bass Drum

Suspended Cymbal

Timpani

Glockenspiel

Looking Down

This bird's-eye picture gives a good view of a percussion section at the back of an orchestra. On the left you can see the timpani. There are four drums of slightly different sizes, each tuned to a different **note**. The drumheads are usually made of plastic. Next to the timpani you can see a bass drum, and a suspended cymbal. On the far right is a glockenspiel. This instrument has metal bars arranged in two rows, each one chiming at a different **pitch** when it is struck with a hard stick.

Tuned Percussion

Trinidad and Tobago is the home of the steel band. During the 1940s, players discovered that steel oil drums could be beaten to make a tuned percussion instrument which produces a wonderful metallic sound when struck. Their cheerful sound has become synonymous with the Caribbean. Each drum, or pan, has different areas tuned to different **pitches**—up to twenty-five on some pans, as few as five on the deepest-pitched pans. The popularity of these bands has spread from the Caribbean to the United States and Europe.

Evelyn Glennie (1965–)

This picture shows the solo percussionist Evelyn Glennie playing a glockenspiel. She was born in Aberdeen, Scotland and went to the Royal Academy of Music in London before starting a hugely successful international career. Her achievements are quite remarkable given that she experienced total hearing loss as a teenager. She has played with many of the world's greatest orchestras and conductors. She has also worked with a **gamelan** *orchestra in Indonesia and a samba band in Brazil, and has written and produced music with the Icelandic pop star Björk.*

• See also pages 35, 59, 74, 91, 114

Have you ever tried blowing across the top of an empty bottle? After some experimenting you may be able to produce a deep hooting sound. The bottle is a very simple pipe, with one closed and one open end. The sound is produced by making the air inside the bottle vibrate. This is how all pipes work, from the simplest panpipe to more complicated modern-day instruments such as the clarinet.

Double Pipes

This man is playing a strange instrument called a double aulos. Some types of folk flutes and folk oboes and clarinets (with **reeds**) have two pipes running side by side, often with one **mouthpiece** at the top. Sometimes one pipe is a **drone**—this means that it sounds a **note** of the same pitch throughout. Sometimes both pipes have **finger holes** so that the player can make more complicated **harmonies**.

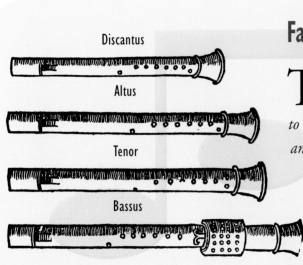

Family of Recorders

Discantus
Altus
Tenor
Bassus

This 16th-century illustration of a family of recorders shows four sizes, ranging from the "discantus" (descant) to the "bassus" (bass). Recorders are usually made from wood, and were very important in the music of the Renaissance and Baroque periods in Western Europe. A group of recorders, called a consort, often included two extra sizes—a smaller instrument called a sopranino, and a very large recorder called the great bass.

← vibrating length of column of air ─────────────

← vibrating length shorter, therefore higher note →

Vibrating Air

When you blow down a pipe the air inside vibrates. The **pitch** of the **note** that sounds depends on the length of the vibrating column of air. A short pipe will produce a higher note than a longer pipe. Many pipes have **finger holes**. These can be covered and uncovered to alter the length of the vibrating column of air, changing the pitch of the note.

Through the Nose

Flutes are most commonly played by blowing air through the mouth, but in some parts of the world the air is blown through the nose. This woman from Malaysia is playing a nose flute. Nose flutes are found across the Pacific and in Southeast Asia. The player often closes one nostril with a thumb, or with a rag, and blows strongly down the other nostril. Many people believe that breath through the nose has special powers of the spirit.

• *See also pages 38*

The pitch of a note is how low or high it sounds. A piccolo plays higher pitched notes than does a tuba or a double bass. Pitch depends on the number of times a sound wave vibrates in a second. This is called the frequency of the sound wave.

Volume in Music

Composers show how loud or soft they want their music to be played by writing instructions in the music. Here are a few of the most common ones:

Marking	Italian name	Meaning
pp	*pianissimo*	very soft
p	*piano*	soft
mp	*mezzo piano*	moderately soft
mf	*mezzo forte*	moderately loud
f	*forte*	loud
ff	*fortissimo*	very loud
cresc.	*crescendo*	getting louder
decresc.	*decrescendo*	getting softer

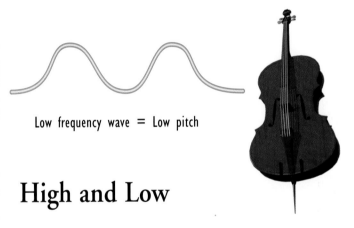

Low frequency wave = Low pitch

High and Low

A sound wave that vibrates many times every second has a high frequency. You hear a high frequency sound wave as a note with high pitch. A sound wave that vibrates fewer times every second has a lower frequency. You hear this sound wave as a lower pitch note. Therefore middle C on the piano has a lower frequency than the G above middle C.

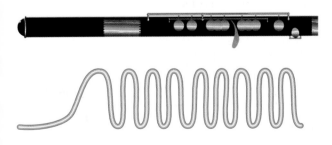

High frequency wave = High pitch

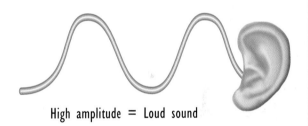

High amplitude = Loud sound

Loud and Quiet

You can play the same note on a musical instrument loudly or quietly. The pitch of the note stays the same, but its volume changes. Volume, or loudness, depends on the strength of the sound wave vibrations. This is called amplitude. The greater the amplitude of the sound wave, the louder the sound.

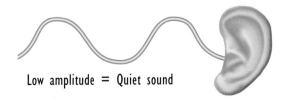

Low amplitude = Quiet sound

• *See also pages 6, 105*

PLUCKED INSTRUMENTS

Many people think that the earliest known musical instrument was the musical bow. This was a hunting bow which gave a twang as it was used to fire an arrow. Since that ancient simple instrument, people have developed **stringed** instruments of all kinds. Many are played by plucking the strings, either with the fingers, or with a piece of hard material called a **plectrum**.

The Sound of the Sitar

This picture shows the Indian musician Ravi Shankar playing the sitar. The sitar is a kind of large Indian lute that is played in the same way as a guitar. It has seven strings that lie over the top of arched metal bars, called **frets**. The player holds down the strings with his fingers to produce different **notes** when the strings are plucked. Beneath the frets are "sympathetic strings." These are not played, but they vibrate when the main strings are sounded, adding a beautiful shimmering effect to the sound.

The Samisen

This photograph, taken in 1900, shows two Japanese dancing women accompanied by the samisen. This long-necked Japanese lute is one of the most popular traditional instruments in Japan. It has a wooden body, covered on the front with animal skin. Its three strings are made from twisted silk. The samisen is played with a plectrum, made from wood.

David the Harpist

This 12th-century religious illustration shows the Biblical King David playing a harp. This small medieval harp was held on the knee. It is known as a frame harp because the wooden frame completely surrounds the strings. The **sound box** is the thickest part of the frame, closest to the player's body. The bible tells us that King David was famous for his beautiful harp playing.

"A Concert"

During the Renaissance period in Western Europe the lute was an extremely popular instrument. This 15th-century painting, called *A Concert*, shows three singers, one of them accompanying their music on the lute. It shows the characteristic shape of the Renaissance lute—a half pear-shaped body and the peg box at the end of the neck bent back at right angles to the **fingerboard**. The lute was used for accompaniment, and also as a solo instrument.

• *See also pages 46-47, 106*

POP MUSIC

Pop music is big business which produces records designed to appeal to the masses. The emphasis is primarily on sales, rather than on creating a lasting musical statement. Pop music is often simple, with a verse and chorus repeated several times. This means that it is easy to listen to, often with catchy tunes. Image is extremely important in pop music, as is catching and inspiring the public mood.

Boy Bands

The Backstreet Boys have been the boy band phenomenon of the last decade. Consisting of Kevin Richardson, Brian Littrell, Howie Dorough, A.J. McLean, and Nick Carter, the band is heavily influenced by the **harmonies** of barbershop and new **rhythm and blues** acts such as Boyz II Men. The Backstreet Boys went on to enjoy

great chart success, first in Europe, then in the United States with hits such as "I'll Never Break Your Heart" and "As Long As You Love Me." Their 1997 album, "Backstreet Boys," went on to sell over 13 million copies, while the follow-ups "Millennium" and "Black and Blue" have ensured their continued success.

Britney Spears

The American teenage singer Britney Spears is the latest example of modern pop, where image is every bit as important as musical content. Whenever Spears enters a studio or concert hall, she has a team of songwriters, stylists, **choreographers**, and publicists behind her. Like her contemporary, Christina Aguillera, she started her showbusiness career with a role on the Mickey Mouse Club, before being groomed for the music world. Her hits include "...Baby One More Time" and "Oops I Did It Again."

Let's Dance

Disco is a type of music with a heavy thump on each beat, designed to dance to. It became hugely popular during the 1970s, and its rise was summed up in the film *Saturday Night Fever*, starring John Travolta. The soundtrack for the film was written by the group the Bee Gees; Barry, Robin, and Maurice Gibb. Other disco stars included Donna Summer, Chic, and towards the end of the disco era, Village People.

Pop Tunes

1. *Waterloo*
   ABBA
2. *Stayin' Alive*
   Bee Gees
3. *Hangin' Tough*
   New Kids On The Block
4. *Heart Of Glass*
   Blondie
5. *Wannabe*
   Spice Girls
6. *Pretty Vacant*
   Sex Pistols
7. *Genie In A Bottle*
   Christina Aguillera
8. *Oops I Did It Again*
   Britney Spears
9. *I'll Be The One*
   Backstreet Boys
10. *ABC*
   Jackson 5

Challenging Pop

The era of punk in the 1970s and '80s challenged the gloss and polish of pop music. This picture shows members of the punk band, the Sex Pistols, in front of Buckingham Palace in London. While the Sex Pistols were the most famous punk band in the UK, the Ramones were the best-known punks in the United States. Their playing stripped music down to its essentials, playing loudly and aggressively. Many people were shocked by the punk movement, but it was a major influence on other bands such as Joy Division and the Clash.

Motown Sensations

Jackie, Tito, Jermaine, Marion, and Michael shot to fame in 1970 with their hit single "I Want You Back." Although they were signed to the Motown label, the Jackson 5 were marketed as a pop band, a musical family led by a talented little boy who could sing and dance. During the early '70s they had a string of hits including "ABC" and "I'll Be There." Michael Jackson was only nine when the group became professional in 1968, but his talent meant that he was quickly singled out as a solo performer, as well as continuing to work with the Jackson 5. He had his first solo number one in the United States in 1972 with "Ben."

• *See also pages 41, 46, 56, 58, 93, 103*

RECORDING MUSIC

The first sound recording was made in 1877 by the American inventor Thomas Alva Edison. During the 20th century, the recording industry had a huge effect on music, as it became possible for people to buy and listen to their favorite recordings in their own homes. Another major revolution was the start of broadcasting in the early 20th century. Today, music can be reproduced accurately using digital technology, so songs can be downloaded through the Internet.

Reaching Millions

Today we take it for granted that we can watch events that are taking place on the other side of the world on our television screens. Global communications mean that huge audiences across the world can all watch the same event at the same time. This picture shows the "Three Tenors": Luciano Pavarotti, Placido Domingo and Jose Carreras in concert in Paris in 1998. This was one of the follow-up concerts to their massive hit-concert at the football World Cup championship in Rome in 1990, when tens of millions of people across the world tuned in to watch this musical event.

Recording Inventions

Edison's invention of 1877 recorded sound on a cylinder covered with tin foil. This machine was called a phonograph. Other inventors were soon working to improve on Edison's machine, and ten years later Emile Berliner invented a device that used discs. This was the gramophone. During the 20th century, research into recording devices continued, resulting in the vinyl disc, cassette tapes, and more recently compact discs (CDs) and digital compact discs (MiniDiscs).

Early Broadcasts

It was an Italian engineer, Guglielmo Marconi, who first succeeded in 1895 in transmitting radio communications. Marconi sent coded telegraph signals, but it was not until the early years of the 20th century that the spoken word was heard on the air waves. By the 1920s most countries had their own radio stations. Among the first was a radio station called W.W.J. in Detroit. Of course, people needed to buy a radio receiver in order to pick up these new radio broadcasts. This poster is for one type of "broadcast-receiver," Radiola.

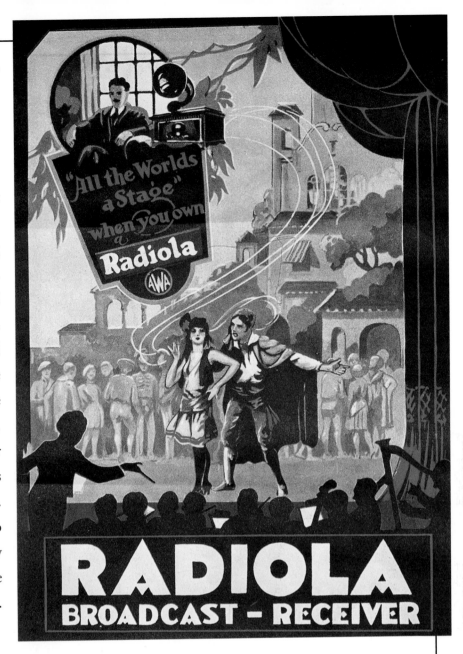

Trumpet Fanfare

These four trumpeters are broadcasting from the B.B.C. studios in England in 1923 as part of Armistice Day. Radio soon began to attract large listening audiences. It had a huge effect on the music industry, as the sounds of all kinds of music, from classical to jazz, were beamed into people's homes. This created a new audience for performers and composers alike. Bandleaders such as Duke Ellington and Glenn Miller soon became big radio stars. The recording industry also boomed, as people bought the latest discs from their favorite stars.

87

• See also pages 65

REGGAE

Reggae music originally came from Jamaica, although it is now well-known all over the world. It is a development of an earlier style of music called **ska**, which became popular in the 1960s. Reggae songs are usually introduced by a short roll on a drum. The speed is slow, and the drum plays an offbeat **rhythm** called a **backbeat** throughout, accompanied by syncopated rhythms on the guitar.

The Specials

The Specials were formed in the UK in 1977 by keyboard player Jerry Dammers. Their style of music was based on a catchy style of dance music coming out of Jamaica in the 1960s called ska. Ska threw a range of styles into the musical melting pot, including **rhythm and blues**, rock 'n' roll, and calypso music. It was typified by spiky, off-beat rhythms. The Specials revived the ska sound in 1979 and mixed it with pop and punk music. It was released on the 2-Tone label which also featured other ska revival bands such as Madness and The Beat. The Specials had several hits including "Gangsters," "A Message to You Rudy" and "Too Much Too Young." Ska music remains popular today, and influences bands in the musical mainstream such as No Doubt.

Out of Jamaica

Reggae was born in Jamaica, a beautiful island in the Caribbean. It takes its influences from a variety of sources including American, African, South American, and Caribbean music. Many reggae singers are Rastafarians, a religion that is widespread in the Caribbean. The lyrics of reggae music explore the plight of the Caribbean's poor and the daily struggles they face.

Bob Marley (1945–1981)

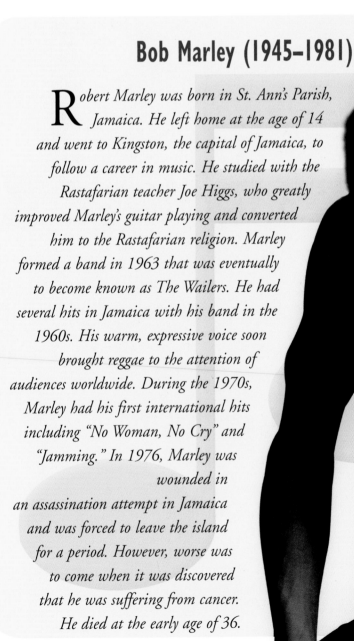

Robert Marley was born in St. Ann's Parish, Jamaica. He left home at the age of 14 and went to Kingston, the capital of Jamaica, to follow a career in music. He studied with the Rastafarian teacher Joe Higgs, who greatly improved Marley's guitar playing and converted him to the Rastafarian religion. Marley formed a band in 1963 that was eventually to become known as The Wailers. He had several hits in Jamaica with his band in the 1960s. His warm, expressive voice soon brought reggae to the attention of audiences worldwide. During the 1970s, Marley had his first international hits including "No Woman, No Cry" and "Jamming." In 1976, Marley was wounded in an assassination attempt in Jamaica and was forced to leave the island for a period. However, worse was to come when it was discovered that he was suffering from cancer. He died at the early age of 36.

• See also page 49

RHYTHM

If you listen carefully to a piece of music, you will quickly notice that notes last for different lengths of time. The combination of notes of different lengths gives music its **rhythm**. Some pieces have a smooth, steady rhythm, while other pieces are more lively, with jumpy, exciting rhythms.

Semibreve	Minim	Crotchet	Quaver	Quavers
4 beats	2 beats	1 beat	½ beat	

Writing Rhythm Down

When monks in medieval times began to write music down, they soon realized that as well as showing the pitch of a note, they also needed to indicate its length. They invented different note shapes to indicate different lengths of note, and this is still how rhythm is written down today. The diagram above shows some of the most common notes and their lengths.

Semibreve rest	Minim rest	Crotchet rest	Quaver rest
4 beats	2 beats	1 beat	½ beat

The Sound of Silence

In every piece of music there are times when an instrument is not playing, or the singer is not singing. These are called rests (shown above). Just like notes, there are different shaped signs to show how long a rest should be.

Playing with Rhythm

Rhythm is just as important in music as pitch. This tabla player can sound only two different pitches on his drums, but the intricate rhythms he plays keep his audience spellbound. Sometimes rhythm deliberately goes against the main pulse of a piece of music. This is called **syncopation**.

● See also pages 27, 49, 55, 61, 66, 68, 91, 94

RITUAL MUSIC

Music has played a vital part in religious ritual from the time of the earliest people. Today music continues to be used in churches, temples, and at ceremonies throughout the world. In many Christian churches, choirs form an important part of worship. The Muslim call to prayer is also an important part of Islam. In Buddhist temples gongs, cymbals, and drums are used to please the gods.

African Rhythms

The drum is an extremely important instrument in Africa, and there are many different kinds played in different regions of this huge continent. This picture shows a ceremonial dance of the Maragoli tribe, near Kakamega, Nigeria. This drummer wears his drum strapped across the body, and beats one end with his hands. Witch doctors in Africa also use drums and other percussion instruments to drive out evil spirits that are plaguing the ill.

A Festival in India

Festivals across the world are usually joyful and colorful events. The Spring festival in India is no exception. This musician is holding a tooteri—a type of wooden horn native to Asia. Religious festivals are an important part of life in India for people of both the Hindu and Muslim faiths. The loud and raucous tones of a **reed** instrument called a shahnai are often heard at outdoor celebrations, particularly in the north of India.

Temple Bell

In Buddist temples in Tibet, young boys are often charged with the responsibility of ringing the bells. Bells are often used as part of worship in temples in the Far East. In Japan, giant bells are hung in special towers in the grounds of Confucian monasteries, and struck with a huge beater swung with the aid of a rope.

Native American Traditions

The musical traditions of the Native Americans go back thousands of years. Healers called shamans use drums and rattles to make contact with the spirit world, while the human voice is important in many ceremonies. Modern Native Americans keep their ancient traditions alive in meetings called powwows, festive gatherings that celebrate their musical inheritance. This Native American dancer is taking part in a modern-day ceremony in Virginia.

• *See also pages 9, 39*

The term "rock" covers many different styles, ranging from indie to grunge and heavy metal. Rock bands are usually made up of electric guitar, bass guitar, and drums, although the line-up varies from band to band. Rock music and pop music come from the same backgrounds, but while rock bands usually place the emphasis on musical talent, pop bands often regard style and image as equally important.

Grunge Rock

Grunge started off as a mixture of heavy metal and punk music, and rose to prominence in the 1990s. It became associated with the city of Seattle, the home of bands such as Green River, Mudhoney, Soundgarden, and Nirvana (right). Nirvana's sound was characterized by sweet melodies washed over with trademark distorted guitar sounds. Nirvana's biggest success was the album "Nevermind" which sold over three million copies in the United States alone.

Sergeant Pepper

The British group The Beatles are one of the most famous groups in the history of rock. The line-up of John Lennon, Paul McCartney, George Harrison, and Ringo Starr came together in 1962, and they had their first United Kingdom number one hit in 1963 with "Please Please Me." In the same year they toured the United States and "Beatlemania" broke out in both countries. The album "Sergeant Pepper's Lonely Heart's Club Band" was recorded in 1967, and is often seen as a landmark in rock history. On it, The Beatles experimented with many different styles, including a **music hall** song "When I'm 64," and played some unusual instruments, such as sitars.

Rock 'n' Roll

Elvis Presley (right) was the first
rock 'n' roll superstar. Heavily influenced
by black musicians such as Little Richard,
he revolutionized popular music with his
energy and hip-swivelling performances.
He brought together many different styles
including country and western, gospel, and old-style
rhythm and blues. His first big hit was "Heartbreak Hotel" in
1956, and it was followed by many more including "Hound Dog" and
"Love Me Tender." Another great rock 'n' roll artist was Buddy Holly who
had hits with "That'll Be The Day" and "Peggy Sue." Buddy Holly died
in a plane crash in 1959, cutting short a promising career.

Heavy Metal

Heavy metal is guitar-led music, characterized by thrashy rhythms, loud
guitars, and growling vocals. One of the most popular heavy metal bands
was Metallica (above). Formed in 1981 in Los Angeles and led by James
Hetfield, they released the album "Master of Puppets" to great acclaim in
1986. It was their 1991 "Metallica" album that helped the band break
through into the mainstream, selling over seven million copies in the United
States alone. Other Heavy Metal bands who have achieved similar levels of
success include Iron Maiden, and more recently, Limp Bizkit and Slipknot,
who have won over many rock fans in America and Europe.

David Bowie (1947–)

David Bowie has been one of the most influential figures in the rock world for the last 30 years. Born David Robert Jones in London, he changed his name from Jones to Bowie in 1966. He had his first hit "Space Oddity" in 1969. In the 1970s he established himself as a glam-rocker both in the United Kingdom and the United States, transforming himself on stage into the character Ziggy Stardust. During a tour of the United States in 1974, Bowie became fascinated by soul music, which influenced the sound of his next album "Young Americans." More hits followed, including "Golden Years," and Bowie also starred in the movie The Man Who Fell To Earth. In the late 1970s, Bowie moved to Berlin and worked with Brian Eno releasing the influential albums "Low" and "Heroes." Bowie had more hits in the 1980s and 90s, and his rock career continues.

In Concert

This picture shows the Rolling Stones in concert at Wembley Stadium, London. The group formed in 1962, and is still giving live concerts today. While The Beatles were clean-cut and unthreatening, the Rolling Stones were always the "bad boys" of rock 'n' roll. Their first transatlantic hit was "I Can't Get No Satisfaction" in 1965. Other smashes included "Ruby Tuesday" and "Paint It Black."

• See also pages 35, 46, 58

SAXOPHONE

The saxophone was invented in the 1840s by a Belgian instrument-maker called Adolphe Sax who worked in Paris. The saxophone is a crossover between brass and woodwind instruments, having a metal body with a clarinet-type mouthpiece and a single reed. It has a deep, soulful sound. There is a whole family of saxophones—the most common sizes in use today are the soprano, alto, tenor, and baritone saxophones.

Origins of the Saxophone

Sax was born in 1814 and died in 1894. He invented the saxophone for use in military bands, but it became very popular in other kinds of music too, especially in jazz. The saxophone makes occasional appearances in the classical orchestra in pieces such as Georges Bizet's "L'Arlisienne."

Made for Jazz

The saxophone has become an extremely important instrument in jazz, prized for its expressive and mellow sound. One of its greatest players was Charlie Parker (left). Born in Kansas City in 1920, Parker taught himself to play the saxophone. In the 1940s, he made several **bebop** recordings with trumpeter Dizzy Gillespie (see page 59). He died at the early age of 34 in 1955.

• See also pages 23, 60

M any people know what a **scale** is from the musical "The Sound of Music," where the characters sing about the solfege syllables Do, Re, Mi, Fa, Sol, La, and Ti. These notes represent the notes in a scale, a pattern of rising or falling notes that move step by step. Most American and European music is based on a system of major or minor scales. Scales are important in music from other traditions, too, including Asia.

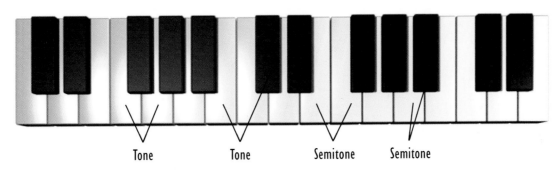

Tone   Tone   Semitone   Semitone

Tones and Semitones

The smallest distance, or interval, between a note and its nearest neighbor in American and European music is called a **semitone**. A step of two semitones is called a **tone**. Scales are the building blocks of music, and are made up of patterns of tones and semitones.

Major Scale

Minor Scale

Pentatonic Scale

Chromatic Scale

Whole Tone

Building Major and Minor scales

To build a **major scale** you move up the scale with this pattern of intervals: tone, tone, semitone, tone, tone, tone, semitone. To build a **minor scale** you move upwards with this pattern of intervals: tone, semitone, tone, tone, semitone, tone and semitone, semitone. Scale defines the piece. There are many different scales apart from major and minor scales. **Pentatonic** scales have just five notes. **Chromatic** scales move semitone by semitone, covering every note on the piano keyboard. **Whole tone** scales move up tone by tone.

Naming Scales

The first **note** of the scale is called the **keynote**. If a piece of music is based on the scale of E minor, it is said to be in the key of E minor.

Ragas

Much Indian music is improvised on scales called **ragas**. There are more than 300 ragas. Some are linked with certain gods and goddesses, some with particular seasons and emotions. Each raga must only be played at a certain time of day. A raga is not based on intervals of **tones** and **semitones** like Western music, but on much smaller intervals called srutis.

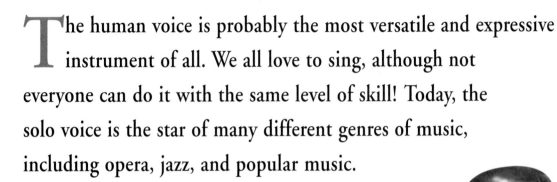

The human voice is probably the most versatile and expressive instrument of all. We all love to sing, although not everyone can do it with the same level of skill! Today, the solo voice is the star of many different genres of music, including opera, jazz, and popular music.

Queen of Jazz

Jazz singer Billie Holiday had a stunning voice and great technical ability. She also sang every song with incredible intensity. Some of her most famous numbers include "Strange Fruit," "Lover Man," and "God Bless The Child." She had a difficult and tragic life, dying in 1959. Her fame increased after her death, and her life story was made into a movie, *Lady Sings The Blues*, starring Diana Ross.

Madonna (1958–)

One of the biggest stars of the pop world is the American singer, Madonna. Born in 1958 in Michigan, Madonna shot to superstardom in the 1980s with hits such as "Like A Virgin" and "Into The Groove." Her success was based on a great singing voice and stunning stage routines. She has appeared in several films since then, most notably as Evita in the film adaptation of Andrew Lloyd Webber's musical Evita. After a brief lull in the mid-1990s, Madonna returned to the top of the charts with the cutting-edge albums "Ray of Light" and "Music."

Frank Sinatra (1915-1998)

Popular crooner Frank Sinatra was brought up in the era of swing bands, and he had the ability to sing in an easy style as well as being a skillful jazz singer. He was heavily influenced by Billie Holiday and recorded a tribute song to her called "Lady Day." He also appeared in more than 50 movies. His greatest hits included "My Way" and "New York, New York."

Opera Singers

Opera singers have to undergo many years of training before their voices are ready to take on large parts, and it is important that they do not strain their voices by singing roles that are unsuitable for them. The American opera singer Barbara Hendricks is known for her beautiful, clear, high voice. She studied at the Juilliard School of Music in New York, and made her debut at the Metropolitan Opera House in 1986, singing the role of Sophie in Richard Strauss's "Der Rosenkavalier."

• See also pages 22, 112, 113

A soloist is someone who stands in front of an audience and performs on their own. Sometimes this means they are entirely alone, without any accompaniment. At other times, the soloist is providing the solo line accompanied by a piano, band, or orchestra. Soloists are usually virtuoso performers whose talent has elevated them to the top of their profession.

The Age of the Virtuosi

The Italian violinist Niccolo Paganini was one of the most exciting and talented violinists ever to appear on the concert platform. He enthralled audiences with his playing in the early 19th century. He was one of many talented players, known as virtuosi, to emerge during the Romantic period. Players such as Franz Liszt and Frederic Chopin, as well as Paganini, also composed music. Their compositions are still played by soloists today.

Kennedy (1956–)

The British violinist, Nigel Kennedy started to play the violin at the age of five. He attended the Sir Yehudi Menuhin School of Music in England and went on to study at the Juilliard School in New York. Kennedy made his debut in London in 1977, playing the violin concerto by Mendelssohn. His groundbreaking recording of Vivaldi's Four Seasons *became the best-selling classical disc of all time. His interest in jazz, rock, and pop music has led him away from the traditional classical repertoire. Since 1997 he has been called simply "Kennedy," and has performed music by rock and pop acts, such as "Light My Fire" by The Doors.*

Jazz Soloists

The famous American jazz trumpeter, Wynton Marsalis, is one in a long line of talented jazz soloists. Marsalis studied at the Juilliard School of Music in New York before starting on a hugely successful jazz career. He is also a renowned classical trumpeter. Other famous solo trumpeters have included Miles Davis, Dizzy Gillespie, and Louis Armstrong.

Music Schools

Many of the famous soloists featured in this book studied at a music school some time in their lives. This picture shows a string group from the famous Juilliard School of Music. Musicians come from all over the world to study with famous teachers at this school.

• *See also pages 15, 23, 53-55, 99, 100, 101, 103, 104, 119*

Soul has its roots in the music sung in churches across the United States by gospel choirs. Based on urban rhythm and blues, soul was created from the addition of more melodic elements drawn from jazz, gospel, and pop music. Soul music is often very rhythmic, with hand-claps or tambourine shakes accompanying voices to accent beats.

A Lasting Influence

Regarded by many as the "Godfather of Soul," James Brown has had as much influence on contemporary music as any other black musician in the late 20th century. Along with Ray Charles, James Brown is credited with turning Rhythm and Blues into soul, and later, "funk." Born in the Deep South, Brown was an exhilarating performer. The word soon spread about his ferocious vocals and on-stage acrobatics, and his shows began to attract thousands. Records like "This Is A Man's World" and "Papa's Got A Brand New Bag" introduced Brown to a global audience. James Brown continues to have an immense influence today, particularly on the hip-hop world, where acts such as Public Enemy sample his work in their own recordings.

Aretha Franklin (1942–)

Aretha Franklin is the queen of soul music. She is responsible for many of the classic soul cuts, from "Respect" and "I Say A Little Prayer" to "I Never Loved A Man." She was a figurehead of Black America in the late '60s and '70s, laying down in music the renewed confidence and pride of a previously disenfranchised generation. Born to a deeply religious family, she grew up surrounded by the gospel tradition, singing in her father's church and making her first recording at the age of fourteen. Although she was courted by Motown, it was at Atlantic Records that her she really began to flourish. Backed up by a strong production team and backing singers who provided a gritty soulfulness to her earthy vocals, she flourished, enjoying ten Top Ten hits in the space of eighteen months.

Otis Redding (1941-1967)

What Motown was doing in Detroit, Stax was doing in Memphis, producing a wealth of soul talent. Otis Redding was one of the most famous artists on the Stax label. He was a master of both the fast dance song and the slow ballad, for example "That's How Strong My Love Is." Sadly he was killed in a plane crash in 1967, just before the release of his last and biggest hit "(Sittin' On) The Dock Of The Bay."

Soul Pioneer

Many people regard Ray Charles as the musician most responsible for developing soul music. He developed this explosive new musical style by combining 1950s **rhythm and blues** with gospel-style vocals, throwing in elements of jazz, blues, and country for good measure. Equally confident on vocals or keyboards, Charles is also renowned for his arrangements. His hits "Drown in My Own Tears" and "The Right Time" paved the way for other soul performers. Today, he continues to draw in huge audiences wherever he performs.

Soul Tunes

1. *Sitting On The Dock Of The Bay*
   Otis Redding
2. *Sweetest Feeling*
   Jackie Wilson
3. *I Want You Back*
   Jackson 5
4. *My Girl*
   Temptations
5. *Tired of Being Alone*
   Al Green
6. *Baby Love*
   Diana Ross & the Supremes
7. *Heard it Through the Grapevine*
   Marvin Gaye
8. *Superstition*
   Stevie Wonder
9. *Respect*
   Aretha Franklin
10. *Walk On By*
    Dionne Warwick

Every sound you hear around you is made by an object vibrating. Watch what happens when a percussion player clashes two cymbals together. The edges of the cymbals move rapidly to and fro, sending out vibrations in the surrounding air. You hear the loud crash as the cymbals hit each other, and then the sound gradually dies away.

Sound Waves

When an object vibrates, it makes the air around it vibrate too. These vibrations are called sound waves. They move outwards in all directions from the vibrating object. When the sound waves reach your ears, you hear the sound.

MUSICAL SOUND   NOISE

Noise and Music

What is the difference between a horrible noise, such as the sound of a drill digging up the road, and a beautiful musical note? The easiest way to find out is to look at the shapes of the sound waves, called waveforms. A tuning fork produces a very clear musical note, and its waveform is very even and smooth. The waveform from a drill would be a jumble of waves, very uneven and irregular.

Hearing

Inside each of your ears is a very thin stretched piece of skin called the eardrum. Sound waves are gathered by the outer ear and move into the ear until they strike the eardrum, making it vibrate. The vibrations are passed deeper into the ear by three small bones, and then to the cochlea. Here they are picked up by nerves which send messages to the brain. This is where the sound is interpreted, allowing you to tell the difference between the wail of a siren and the bark of a dog.

105

• *See also pages 6, 81*

STRING FAMILY

The **string** family is made up of the violin, viola, cello, double bass, and harp. All these instruments produce sound by making a string vibrate, either with a bow, or by plucking the string.

Making a Bow

Violins, violas, cellos, and double basses are played by drawing a bow across the strings. The bow is a similar design for all these instruments, but those used for the cello and double bass are shorter and heavier than the bows used for the violin and viola. The wooden part of the bow is usually made from Brazil wood, which is heated in order to give it a curve. The hair of the bow is horse hair, taken from the tails of horses. Each bow has about 200 strands of hair. The hair is tightened and loosened by turning a screw, called the frog, at the bottom end of the bow.

The String Section

The string section is by far the largest section of the classical orchestra. As well as cellos, double basses, and violas, the modern orchestra has up to thirty violins, divided into first and second sections. The string players sit in ranks, called desks, usually two to a music stand. The violin player on the front desk nearest the conductor is known as the concert master.

Seating of a modern orchestra

The string section sits at the front of the orchestra. The violins are usually on the left, violas in the middle, and cellos and double basses on the right, although this arrangement can change depending on the music being played.

Violins

Harp

Violas

Cellos

Double Bass

Electric Strings

This unusual shaped violin is an electric violin. But like a normal violin, sound is produced by drawing a bow over the four strings. The difference lies in the way that the sound is made louder, or amplified. In a normal violin, the vibrations of the strings are picked up by the air inside the body of the violin, amplifying the sound of the vibrations. This electric violin does not need a body because the vibrations are picked up by electric attachments and amplified through a loudspeaker.

TEMPO

Have you ever listened to your own heartbeat, or the ticking of a clock? These sounds have a steady, repetitive pulse. Music often has a pulse, or beat, too. Sometimes the beat is slow and stately. Sometimes it is faster and more lively. The speed of a piece of music is called its **tempo**.

How Many Beats?

The steady beats of a piece of music are grouped together, often in groups of two, three, or four beats. When music is written down on the staff, these groups are indicated by lines, called bar lines. The bar lines divide the music up into measures. At the beginning of a piece of music, you will see two numbers, one above the other. This is the **time signature**. The top number tells you how many beats there are in each measure. The bottom number tells you the value in time of each beat.

Tempo Terms

Composers can also indicate how quickly or slowly they want their music to be played by writing certain words in the music. Here are a few of the most common terms:

Italian word	Meaning
lento	slow
adagio	quite slow
moderato . . .	at a moderate pace
allegro	fast
vivace	fast and lively
presto	very fast

Picking the Tempo

One of the jobs of the conductor is to indicate the tempo of a piece to the orchestra. The musicians in the orchestra need to know how fast or slow the pulse of a piece of music will be before they start to play. Composers sometimes indicate the tempo of a piece of music by showing how many beats there should be in a minute. This picture shows Kurt Masur conducting the New York Philharmonic orchestra.

• *See also pages 61, 68-69, 81, 90*

The trombone was developed from an older instrument called the sackbut. The tuba is a much younger instrument—the first tubas were made in the 1830s in Germany. Both instruments are important members of the orchestral brass section, as well as brass bands. The trombone also appears in many jazz groups.

Playing the Tuba

The tuba provides the bass line of the brass section. There are three sizes of tuba commonly played in the orchestra. For brass bands, where the tuba sometimes has to be played on the march, there is a marching tuba (shown right). This version is held on the shoulder. The bell is made from fiberglass instead of metal to make the instrument lighter and easier to carry.

Playing the Trombone

The trombone is unlike the other brass instruments in having a slide valve. The player lengthens or shortens the vibrating column of air inside the tube by pushing and pulling the slide in and out. There are seven different positions for the slide; the lowest note is sounded when the slide is pushed out farthest. The slide allows the trombonist to produce some amazing sounds, including a "sliding" glissando effect.

• See also pages 16, 17, 59, 60

TRUMPET

The trumpet is the oldest member of the orchestral brass section. Trumpets date back to ancient times, and for thousands of years their bright tones have been the sound of pageantry and ceremony. Early trumpets were long, straight tubes (still used today for ceremonial purposes), but modern orchestral trumpets are folded up to make a more compact instrument with the same brilliant sound.

Solo Trumpets

Modern-day trumpets are used in the orchestra, where they are often given solo lines. The trumpet player uses the three **valves** and the **mouthpiece** to vary the pitch of the notes. Trumpets create a dazzling sound, and are often used for fanfares and signals, as well as in classical and jazz music.

Natural to Valve

Early trumpets were "natural" trumpets. This means that the player could only sound a limited range of notes depending on the length of the tube. This is why trumpets were used for playing fanfares, musical flourishes based on a few different pitches. In the 1820s, valves were first introduced on trumpets. Valves control the flow of air, thus allowing players to play a greater variety of notes. Modern trumpets have three valves.

• See also pages 16, 17, 38, 52, 102

The violin is a very popular and versatile instrument. Its agility and beautiful tone make it ideal as a solo instrument. But it is also a vital part of the classical orchestra, where many violins play the same part of music together. The viola is slightly larger than the violin, with a darker and more mellow tone.

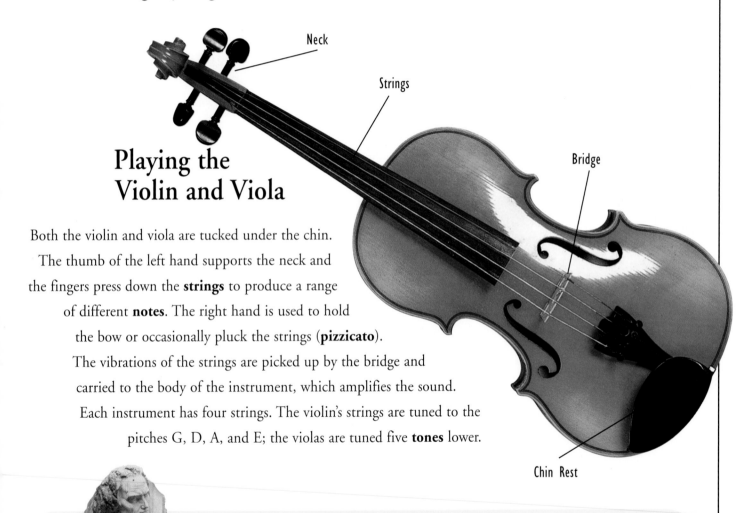

Neck

Strings

Bridge

Chin Rest

Playing the Violin and Viola

Both the violin and viola are tucked under the chin. The thumb of the left hand supports the neck and the fingers press down the **strings** to produce a range of different **notes**. The right hand is used to hold the bow or occasionally pluck the strings (**pizzicato**). The vibrations of the strings are picked up by the bridge and carried to the body of the instrument, which amplifies the sound. Each instrument has four strings. The violin's strings are tuned to the pitches G, D, A, and E; the violas are tuned five **tones** lower.

ANTONIO STRADIVARI

Antonio Stradivari (1644–1737)

Antonio Stradivari is renowned for his stringed instruments, especially violins. He lived and worked in Cremona, Italy, where he worked for another violin-maker, Niccolo Amati, until the 1660s. Stradivari's instruments were highly-regarded in his own lifetime for their beautiful yet powerful tone. Today, they are sold for hundreds of thousands of dollars.

111

• See also pages 20, 34, 106

VOICE

The human voice is a natural musical instrument, used to express a whole range of emotions. There are countless numbers of different styles of singing, from opera to folk, pop, and rock. Some require only a limited degree of musical expertise, while styles like opera require many years of practice to perfect.

The voicebox

Your larynx, or voicebox, is situated in your throat. The larynx contains your vocal cords, which vibrate when air passes over them, producing the sound of speech, or singing. When your voice chords are pulled tight, a high note is produced. When they are relaxed and loose, a lower note is produced. The flow of air across your vocal cords is controlled by the large muscle beneath your lungs, called the diaphragm. Women tend to have shorter vocal chords than men, which is why they have higher singing voices.

Mouth

Larynx

Diaphragm   Lungs   Windpipe

The Art of Singing

However good the voice, most singers need a microphone to amplify their voice when performing for an audience. The microphone turns the vibrations of the voice into electrical pulses, and then makes them louder. The sound of the voice is then fed out through loudspeakers. This type of singing is very different from singing without any amplification. Opera singers have to learn to sing without the help of microphones, using the natural power of their voices to fill a large opera house or concert hall.

Singing Madrigals

This picture dates from 1568 and shows a group of men and women gathered around a table to sing madrigals. A madrigal was a piece written usually for three to eight voices, each voice singing a different part. They were very popular in 16th-century Italy and England. They were often published in separate parts, so that people could sit around a table, reading their own part.

The *Haka*

These Maoris are performing a traditional dance called the *haka*. Maoris are the original peoples of New Zealand and the *haka* is their traditional war chant. Before the arrival of white settlers in New Zealand, the Maoris had no written language, but they used singing and poetry to pass on stories and poems from one generation to another. The *haka* is a reminder of this time, when the voice was used together with body movements to convey a clear warning to potential enemies.

People all over the world have been inventing and adapting musical instruments for thousands of years. In theatres, people have used a range of strange instruments to imitate the sounds of the weather, animals, and other sounds. Weird instruments also find their way into percussion sections of modern orchestras.

The "Kitchen Sink Department"

The percussion section of the classical orchestra is sometimes known as the "kitchen sink department" because all sorts of odd instruments find their place here. Some of these odd instruments include typewriters, chains, anvils, sirens, and popguns. Pictured here is a metal thunder sheet, used to create a sound like wind and thunder.

Roaring Sound

This bull-roarer comes from Australia. Bull-roarers date back more than 25,000 years. To play a bull-roarer you whirl it fast around your head. You can change the pitch of the sound produced by whirling slightly faster or slower. In ancient times, the sound of the bull-roarer was thought to protect against evil spirits.

The Stroh Fiddle

This gypsy fiddler is playing a Stroh fiddle, invented by a German engineer called Augustus Stroh. This strange violin has a shallow wooden body with a metal horn attached. The vibrations of the strings are transmitted through the bridge of the violin to a lever, and the vibrations are picked up and made louder by the horn. When it was first played, it was described as having a sound "as loud as four violins."

WOODWIND FAMILY

The woodwind family is made up of the flute, oboe, clarinet, and bassoon. Some woodwind instruments are made of wood, others of metal. But they all produce sound in various ways when air is blown through them.

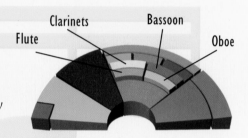

Woodwind Position

The woodwind section sits in the middle of the orchestra. The flutes and oboes are usually in front of the clarinets and bassoons.

Flute Clarinets Bassoon Oboe

Instrument-maker

This man is working on an oboe in an instrument factory. The oboe is mounted on a lathe, and you can see some of its keys between the maker's two hands. The oboe, like the clarinet and bassoon, is made from wood, often African blackwood. It is made in three sections that can be pulled apart when the instrument is not being played and stored in a case.

Woodwind Section

The woodwind section is usually relatively small. There are two or three players of each instrument.
These are solo instruments which often have music parts that are heard above the rest of the orchestra.
Many of the woodwind instruments have bigger or smaller relations. They include the piccolo, a small version
of the flute, the *cor anglais*, related to the oboe, and the double- or contra-bassoon, which is a larger version
of the bassoon with a very deep sound.

WORLD MUSIC

World music is a term that has been used in the last 15 years or so to describe a wide variety of music. It covers everything from Hungarian folk music to calypso, klezmer, and Afro-beat. Interest in world music has opened up many ears to the varied and wonderful sounds of music from the farthest corners of the planet.

Gypsy Music

Wandering communities such as gypsies often have a proud musical tradition, handing down songs and musical techniques through the generations. This gypsy man is playing a fiddle. Today, many gypsies have settled down to live in one place. In central Europe, in countries such as Hungary and Romania, gypsy bands are well-known. Some of these bands include unusual instruments such as cimbaloms, stringed instruments that are played by striking the strings with hard beaters.

Yossou N'Dour (1968–)

Born in Senegal, Yossou N'Dour started performing when he was twelve years old, and formed his own band, Etoile de Dakar, in 1977. His style of music is known as mbalax, and it is a mixture of African, Caribbean, and pop styles. The rhythms of mbalax and N'Dour's beautiful voice brought a series of hits during the 1980s. He now has his own recording studio, Studio Xippi, at home in Dakar in Senegal. N'Dour has recorded with American and European pop stars such as Sting and Bruce Springsteen. N'Dour had his biggest hit, "Seven Seconds," with the British singer Nehneh Cherry.

Afro-beat

Fela Kuti was the man who invented Afro-beat. Born in Nigeria in 1938, his parents sent him to Britain to study to become a doctor. But Fela took a course at the Trinity College of Music in London instead. He formed his own band called Koola Lobitos, reforming it under the same name when he returned to Nigeria in 1963. His music combined influences of traditional African music with jazz and highlife (a type of West African dance music), and he named it Afro-beat. Fela Kuti had many Afro-beat hits during the 1970s and increasingly attacked the Nigerian military government through his music. He was put in prison in 1985 but released two years later after worldwide protests.

GLOSSARY

Acoustic
A music instrument that is played without any electric amplification

Backbeat
Beat played on the second or fourth beats of music written in even time, or the last beat in more complicated time signatures

Bar
A single measure in music

Chanter
A pipe on a set of bagpipes that has finger holes

Chord
The sounding of two or more musical notes at the same time

Choreographer
Person responsible for the arrangement of dance steps to music

Chromatic Scale
A musical scale that ascends and descends in semitones

Counterpoint
A piece of music where two or more parts are sounded simultaneously

Crook
Tubing added to a wind instrument to obtain a lower tone

Drone
Single reed pipe on a bagpipe, accompanying the tune played on the chanter

Ensemble
A small group of musicians performing together

Finger holes
Holes on a wind instrument that are covered or uncovered to vary the pitch of the note that is sounded

Fingerboard
The long strip of hardwood on a stringed instrument upon which the strings are stopped by the fingers

Flat
A musical sign that indicates a note is to be lowered by a semitone

Frame Drum
Drum skin stretched over a thin, shallow frame

Fret
A small metal bar on the fingerboard of a stringed instruments

Gamelan
Percussion orchestra commonly found in East Asia

Glissando	The shimmering effect produced by a series of notes being played in rapid succession
Glockenspiel	A percussion instrument made up of a series of tuned metal bars
Harmony	A combination of agreeable musical notes sounded at the same time
Holler	A field chant commonly sung by slaces on plantations in the American south
Key	The main tonal center in a musical composition
Keynote	The note upon which a scale or piece of music is based
Larynx	Organ in the human body that contains the vocal chords
Major Scale	A scale where each interval is separated by a whole tone, except for the third and fourth degrees, and the seventh and eighth degrees, which are separated by a semitone
Mbiri	An African musical instrument also known as the thumb piano, made up of tuned metal strips attached to a sound box
Melody	A succession of notes that form a tune
MIDI	The language through which computers can talk to electric musical instruments
Minor Scale	A scale where the second, third, fifth, and sixth notes are separated by a semitone
Mouthpiece	The device on a wind instrument through which the player blows to sound a note
Music Hall	Also known as vaudeville, this is variety entertainment made up of a mixture of songs and comic acts
Notation	The language in which musical pieces are written down
Note	A single sound from a musical instrument

GLOSSARY

Octave   *Interval of eight notes between two notes, one of which has twice the pitch of the other*

Opera   *Productions where dramatic stories are set to music*

Operetta   *A comic or lighthearted opera*

Pentatonic   *A scale consisting of just five notes*

Pickups   *The electrical device on a musical instrument that converts vibrations into electric signals*

Pitch   *The frequency of a musical note*

Plectrum   *Object used for plucking a stringed instrument*

Raga   *Patterns of melody and rhythm used in Indian music*

Reed   *A thin piece of metal or cane that is attached to the mouthpiece of a woodwind instrument, producing a sound when it vibrates*

Rhythm   *The arrangement of various durations of notes in a piece of music*

Sampling   *Process by which a computer can be used to take in a sound and play it back in a number of different ways*

Scale   *A sequence of musical notes arranged in ascending or descending order*

Scat   *Style of jazz singing where improvised nonsense sounds are sung instead of real words*

Scratching   *Technique used in hip-hop where a needle is stopped on a record and moved back and forward by the D.J., creating a harsh, abrasive sound*

Sea Shanty   *A rhythmical song sung by sailors often while they worked*

Semitone   *A musical interval that is half a tone; the distance between one note and its flattened or sharpened equivalent*

Sharp	*Musical sign that is used to raise a note by a semitone*
Ska	*A style of Caribbean pop music where the second and fourth beats of a four beat bar are accented*
Slit drums	*Drum made out of a hollow piece of wood, played by striking with a beater*
Sound box	*The resonating box of the hollow body of a musical instrument such as a violin*
Srati	*Musical interval in Indian music which is less than a semitone*
Staff	*Group of five horizontal lines upon which musical notes are written*
Strings	*A stretched wire or chord used in stringed instruments to produce a sound*
Symphony	*An extended composition for a large orchestra, made up of several movements*
Syncopation	*The accent of the weak beats (second and fourth beats) in music, as opposed to the strong beats (first and third)*
Tempo	*The speed at which a musical composition is played*
Tone	*A musical interval comprised of two semitones*
Triad	*A three-note chord*
Time Signature	*A graphic device at the start of a piece of music consisting of two figures; the upper figure indicating how many beats per bar, the lower figure the value of each beat*
Valve	*Mechanical device on a brass instrument used to alter the length of the column of air inside, thus changing the pitch produced*
Whole Tone Scale	*A scale where each note in the sequence is a whole tone apart*

INDEX

ACKNOWLEDGMENTS

We would like to thank Rod Teasdale and Elizabeth Wiggans for their help with this book, the following picture agencies for permission to reproduce their material in this book, Roddy Paine Studios for additional photography, and John Alston for the artwork.

t=top, b=bottom, c=center, l=left, r=right, OFC=front cover

AKG; 18cr, 19cl, 25t, 26t, 27b, 29b, 38t, 38b, 60t, 69cr, 75t, 83t, 86bl, 101r. Art Archive; 20t, 87r. Corbis; 6l, 10br, 11t, 11bl, 36b, 39r, 36b, 54t, 59c, 62b, 86l, 106t. Hulton Getty; 87b. Kobal Collection; 50b, 66cl, 85tl, 100tl. Lebrecht; 7b, 8t, 8b, 9t, 9b, 13cl, 14b, 15t, 16b, 17t, 17b, 18b, 19b (Farrell), 21c, 22b (Four), 23r, 24t, 24b, 25b, 26b, 27t, 29t (Mount), 30cl, 32b (Highet), 33cl (Haywood), 34cr, 36t, 41c, 42t, 42b, 43c, 44t (Highet), 44b, 44–45c, 47cl, 47cr, 48c (Mount), 51t, 51b (Noel), 53cl, 53cr, 55t, 55b (Minnion), 56c (Salter), 57cl, 64bl, 65b (Robert), 67cl, 68c, 69c, 71cl (Smith), 72t, 72b, 73t, 73b, 74 (Lauterwasser), 75b (Noel, 77b (Luekhust), 78 (Del Mer), 79t, 79b, 82c (Farrell), 83cr, 83b, 86cr (Hughton), 90bl (Peric), 91br (Naranha), 96b (Tree), 98c (Noel), 99r, 100cr (Salter), 101cl, 102t, 102b (Wales), 106b (Wales), 106–107c (Peric), 108b, 111b, 113t, 114c, 115t (Stock), 115b (Salter), 116b (Salter), 117c (Four), 118c. Mary Evans; 60b. Performing Arts; 22, 82b, 91t. Pictor; 33r, 77cl, 78t, 91t. Redferns; 62cr, 63t, 63b, 84t, 85b, 89br, 92b, 103t, 103b, 105b. Rex; 7t, 28l, 59r, 66b, 85c, 92t, 95t, 95b, 113b, 119b. Ronald Grant; 30t, 31t, 45b, 49t, 49b, 52c, 64c, 67r, 88c, 93t, 93b, 94t, 96t, 119t. Tony Stone; 76c. Werner Forman; 41c.